MEXICAN WOLF RECOVERY: THREE-YEAR PROGRAM REVIEW AND ASSESSMENT[1]

I0500424

Prepared by the Conservation Breeding Specialist Group (CBSG), Apple Valley, Minnesota; for the United States Fish and Wildlife Service, Albuquerque, New Mexico:

PAUL C. PAQUET
UNIVERSITY OF CALGARY &
CONSERVATION SCIENCE INC.

JOHN A. VUCETICH
MICHIGAN TECHNOLOGICAL UNIVERSITY

MICHAEL K. PHILLIPS
TURNER ENDANGERED SPECIES FUND

LEAH M. VUCETICH
MICHIGAN TECHNOLOGICAL UNIVERSITY

Conservation Breeding Specialist Group
12101 Johnny Cake Ridge Road
Apple Valley, MN 55124-8151
tel: 1-952-997-9800
e-mail: office@cbsg.org
June 2001

---

[1]**Recommended Citation:** Paquet, P C , Vucetich, J , Phillips, M L , and L Vucetich 2001   Mexican wolf recovery: three year program review and assessment   Prepared by the Conservation Breeding Specialist Group for the United States Fish and Wildlife Service 86 pp

ACKNOWLEDGMENTS

We thank Onnie Byers and Linda Phillips for their help in preparing this document. Wendy Brown, Daniel Groebner, and Brian Kelley promptly provided the biological information necessary for our review. We are particularly grateful to the Interagency Field Team, Interagency Management Advisory Group, and David Parsons for advising us about the details of the Mexican wolf reintroduction program. Lastly, we thank the San Carlos Apache Nation for hosting a meeting with individuals and organizations involved with reintroduction of Mexican wolves.

TABLE OF CONTENTS

LIST OF FIGURES

LIST OF TABLES

1. INTRODUCTION

Herein we assess the progress of efforts to reestablish Mexican wolves *(Canis lupus baileyi)* in the Blue Range Wolf Recovery Area (BRWRA). This review is a direct result of an Environmental Impact Statement (EIS) concluded by the U.S. Fish and Wildlife Service (USFWS) in 1996 (U.S. Fish and Wildlife Service 1996). The EIS and associated final rule (Parsons 1998) call for the USFWS to reestablish Mexican wolves to the BRWRA. The recovery area encompasses 17,752 km² (6,854 mi²) of the Apache National Forest in southeastern Arizona and the Gila National Forest in southwestern New Mexico.

Specifically, the U.S. Department of Interior has authorized the USFWS to reintroduce about 15 wolves every year for 3 to 5 years in the BRWRA primary recovery zone. The primary recovery zone comprises about 2,664 km² (1,029 mi²) of the Apache National Forest (Groebner *et al.* 1995). The remainder of the Apache National Forest and all the Gila National Forest make up the secondary recovery zone. The USFWS may conduct re-releases in the secondary recovery zone and wolves that move from the primary recovery zone can inhabit the secondary zone.

The USFWS began reintroductions with the release of 11 wolves in March 1998. From then until March 2001 the USFWS released another 45 individuals on 61 occasions. An Interagency Field Team comprising employees from the USFWS, Wildlife Services (U.S. Department of Agriculture), Arizona Department of Game and Fish, and New Mexico Department of Game and Fish carried out the releases and associated fieldwork

The final rule governing the reintroduction project (Parsons 1998) and the 1998 Mexican Wolf Interagency Management Plan both require the USFWS to conduct a comprehensive review of the project at the end of the third year (i.e., March 2001). The full evaluation must include recommendations regarding continuation, modification, or cancellation of the reintroduction effort. If appropriate, the evaluation may include recommendations on whether and how to use the White Sands Wolf Recovery Area.

The primary goal of the reintroduction effort is to restore a self-sustaining population of about 100 wild Mexican wolves distributed over 12,950 km² (5,000 mi²) of the BRWRA. Such an objective is consistent with the 1982 Mexican Wolf Recovery Plan (U.S. Fish and Wildlife Service 1982 (EIS). The 1998 Mexican Wolf Interagency Management Plan projects that about 9 years will be required to achieve this objective. Wolves in the BRWRA are to be managed to reduce negative impacts and maximize positive influences on the lifestyles and economy of local residents.

The USFWS contacted the Conservation Breeding Specialist Group (CBSG) to conduct the specified review. CBSG is ideally suited for the task because of extensive worldwide experience with small population restoration, conservation, and management. On behalf of CBSG, Paul Paquet assembled an expert review team composed of John Vucetich, Michael Philips, and Leah Vucetich. The team review is based on data provided by the USFWS data collected in the first 3 years of the reintroduction project.

2.   ISSUES FOR WHICH ASSESSMENTS WERE REQUESTED

Our assessment addresses the following questions as outlined by the 1998 Mexican Wolf Interagency Management Plan.

- ▸ Have wolves successfully established home ranges within the designated wolf recovery area?
- ▸ Have reintroduced wolves reproduced successfully in the wild?
- ▸ Is wolf mortality substantially higher than projected in the EIS?
- ▸ Is population substantially growth lower than projected in the EIS?
- ▸ Are numbers and vulnerability of prey are adequate to support wolves?
- ▸ Is the livestock depredation control program effective?
- ▸ Have documented cases of threats to human safety occurred?

We were not asked to address the following 2 additional questions identified in the 1998 Mexican Wolf Interagency Management Plan:

- ▸ Is effective cooperation occurring with other agencies and the public?
- ▸ Are combined agency funds and staff adequate to carry out needed management, monitoring and research?

3. OUR APPROACH

Although a paucity of data compels us to speculate on many biological issues, we do so using the best available information about wolf ecology. The lack of information reflects the short time the Program has been underway. Where necessary and appropriate we infer from published studies conducted elsewhere, our own experiences, and the experience of other researchers and managers. Throughout the report, we are careful to distinguish fact from inference, speculation, and professional opinion. Our conclusions and recommendations reflect our current knowledge and the fundamental principles of Conservation Biology.

Conclusions and recommendations depend on the likelihood of the assumptions underlying the assessment. Therefore, we reviewed several principles of conservation biology, which apply to restoring and maintaining a viable population of wolves. Some of these principles are established generalizations, some are testable hypotheses, and others are practical guides that we assessed as important in developing our recommendations.

- ▸ The fewer data or more uncertainty involved, the more conservative conclusions must be
- ▸ To be comprehensive, an assessment must be concerned with multiple levels of biological organizations and with many different spatial and temporal scales.
- ▸ Species well distributed across their native range are less susceptible to extinction than species confined to small portions of their range.
- ▸ Large blocks of habitat containing large populations of a target species are superior to small blocks containing small populations.
- ▸ Maintaining viable ecosystems is usually more efficient, economical, and effective than a species by species approach.
- ▸ Viability of wild populations depends on the maintenance of ecological processes.
- ▸ Human disturbances that mimic or simulate natural disturbances are less likely to threaten restoration efforts than disturbances radically different from the natural regime.

We note that how we measure and perceive the success or failure of wolf recovery is contextual. Accordingly, our focus is on wolf ecology and how the quality of management affects the persistence of the reintroduced Mexican wolf population. Specifically, we are concerned with the viability of the population as affected by habitat quality, population size, population isolation, and agency management. Although a viable wolf population could affect people's lives and the economy, we do not consider social and economic issues in this report.

Finally, our protocol for assessment was to:
- ▸ Review pertinent scientific literature
- ▸ Use available data provided by the Interagency Field Team
- ▸ Review pertinent regulations, polices, and rules
- ▸ Evaluate data quality
- ▸ Identify data gaps
- ▸ Analyze and interpret data

- ▸　　Compare progress with program goals
- ▸　　Evaluate program success & failures
- ▸　　Develop data collection, data management & conservation recommendations

4. ECOLOGICAL BACKGROUND

a. RESILIENCY

Resilience has been defined as the ability to absorb disturbance and still maintain the same relationship between populations or state variables (Holling 1973) and the degree to which an entity can be changed without altering its minimal structure (Pickett *et al.* 1989). Thus, resilience can be thought of as a property of a system, whereas persistence is the outcome (Weaver *et al.* 1996).

Wolves evolved in environments that included prevailing disturbance regimes with certain ecological characteristics and boundary conditions. Disturbance varied in frequency, duration, extent, and intensity, thereby resulting in different spatio-temporal patterns of change. Behaviors and life history traits conferred resilience that enabled wolves to absorb these intrinsic disturbances and persist. Modern humans, however, have presented new regimes of disturbance that could be considered exotic because they are qualitatively novel or quantitatively atypical.

Three mechanisms of resilience at different hierarchical levels are: individual - plasticity in foraging behavior that ameliorates flux in food availability; population - demographic compensation that mitigates increased exploitation; and metapopulation dispersal - that provides functional connectivity among fragmented populations. Accordingly, flexible food habits, high annual productivity, and dispersal capabilities enable wolves to respond to natural and human-induced disturbances (Weaver *et al.* 1996). However, environmental disturbances at various temporal and spatial scales may exceed the ability of wolves and systems that support them to absorb disturbance (Weaver *et al.* 1996).

Wolves display remarkable behavioral plasticity in using different prey and habitats (Mech 1991). They are able to substitute one resource for another in the face of environmental disturbance (Weaver *et al.* 1996). Specifically, wolves specialize on vulnerable individuals of large prey [elk (*Cervus elaphus*) and moose (*Alces alces*)] yet readily generalize to common prey [usually deer (*Odocoileus sp.*)] (Weaver *et al.* 1996).

Wolf populations are able to compensate demographically for excessive mortality. Under certain circumstances this compensation enables wolves to respond to increased rates of juvenile or adult mortality with increased reproduction and/or survival, thereby mitigating demographic fluctuations (Weaver *et al.* 1996). Dominant wolves are able to reproduce at a very young age and usually reproduce every year thereafter (Weaver *et al.* 1996). Age at reproductive senescence has not been well documented but few females survive to reproduce past age 9 (Mech 1988). Wolves also display remarkable ability to recover from exploitation. For example, during a wolf reduction program in the Yukon, wolves recovered to pre-reduction densities within 5 years (Hayes and Harestad 2000). Wolves immigrated into the study area during early recovery, followed by increases in pack size from reproduction (Hayes *et al.* 2000).

The final mechanism that confers resilience to wolf populations is dispersal. When dispersal is successful, vanishing local populations are rescued from extirpation (Brown and Kodric-Brown 1977) and functional connectivity of metapopulations is established (Hansson 1991). Wolves have tremendous dispersal capabilities and as a result, "connectivity" of populations can be high. Dispersing wolves typically establish territories or join packs within 50-

100 km of the pack in which they were born (Fritts and Mech 1981, Fuller 1989, Gese and Mech 1991, Wydeven *et al.* 1995, Boyd *et al.* 1996). Some wolves, however, move longer distances. For example, Fritts (1983) observed a wolf that traveled at least 917 km.

b.   THE PERILS OF SMALL POPULATIONS

Small populations, because of random normal variability in demographics, are more likely to become extinct than larger populations (Schonewald-Cox *et al.* 1983). Moreover, these small populations are thought to be vulnerable because of deleterious effects of inbreeding (Wright 1977) and chance environmental disturbances such as forest fires, disease or infestations that affect a species or its prey (Franklin 1980). In theory, the interaction of these factors increases the probability of extinction (Shafer 1987).

Small insular populations may have a restriction of genetic variation because they represent a very small subset of the total population (i.e., a few individuals). As populations become smaller a further reduction in genetic variation results in decreased survival (i.e., increased mortality). Increased mortality leads to additional reduction in genetic variation resulting in an "extinction vortex." Biologists theorize that because of this self-amplifying cycle the rate of extinction for small populations is higher than predicted from the population size alone (cf. Caro and Laurenson 1994).

c.   USE OF HABITAT AND PATTERNS OF TRAVEL

Throughout its broad geographical distribution the gray wolf is considered an ecosystem and prey generalist. However, populations are adapted to local conditions and are, therefore, specialized concerning den site use, foraging habitats, and prey selection. In mountain regions, the effects of physiography, weather, prey distribution, and prey abundance combine to concentrate activities of wolves into forested valley bottoms (Paquet 1993, Paquet *et al.* 1996, Paquet *et al.* 1996, Weaver 1994, Singleton 1995, and others).

Elevation can also govern seasonal movements of wolves. In mountainous areas with high snowfall, use of low elevation valleys increases during winter, where frozen rivers and lakes, shorelines, and ridges are preferred because of ease of travel. Ski trails, snowmobile trails, graded roads, and packed roads can artificially enhance the range and efficiency of winter forays (Paquet 1993). Singleton (1995) has suggested that variation in pack size, variation in home range size, and interactions with sympatric predators may influence habitat use and travel patterns. He further speculated that turning frequency or travel route complexity are likely to vary depending on whether an animal is within a patch of concentrated resource availability (e.g., deer winter ranges), moving between known patches, or exploring new areas.

d.   INFLUENCE OF WOLVES ON THE BIOLOGICAL COMMUNITY

Generally we understand that the ecology of predators, prey, and scavengers, is intertwined. However, the details of these relationships, and the general role of predation in shaping the structure of ecological communities is poorly understood. Changes in predator-prey relationships may affect species other than wolves and their prey. Disruption of top predators can affect interspecific associations by disrupting relationships within food webs. This, in turn, may cause unanticipated ripple effects in populations of other species (Paine 1966, 1969, 1980;

Terborgh and Winter 1980, Frankel and Soulé 1981, Wilcox and Murphy 1985, Wilcove *et al.* 1986, Valone and Brown 1995), which markedly alter the diversity and composition of a community (Paine 1966). Multi species effects often occur when changes in a third species mediate the effect of one species on a second species (or analogous higher-order interactions). For example, a wolf can affect a grizzly bear (*Ursus arctos*) by reducing the availability of a limiting resource (possibly an ungulate). Also a secondary carnivore such as a coyote (*C. latrans*) can affect the degree to which a herbivore's lifestyle is influenced by a primary carnivore such as a wolf. Ecologists have only begun to develop theory that attempts to explain the coexistence of prey in terms of predator-influenced niches ("enemy-free space").

Terborgh and Winter (1980) noted that we know little about the loss of top carnivores in terrestrial environments, and predicted a wave of extinctions following the loss of any key species. For example, if species interact as competitors, as predator and prey, or as facilitators in successional processes, then the presence of one species may influence the extinction probability of another "linked" species.

Recent evidence suggests the importance of cascading trophic interactions on terrestrial ecosystem function and processes. Research has documented differences within systems from which large predators have been removed or are missing (Glanz 1982, Emmons 1984, Terborgh 1988, Leigh *et al.* 1993, Terborgh *et al.* 1999). Accordingly, the ecosystem impacts of wolves may be more profound than previously expected. For example, on Isle Royale, Michigan wolf predation on moose has been shown to influence positively biomass production in trees of boreal forest (McLaren and Peterson 1994). Growth rates of balsam fir (*Abies balsamea*) were regulated by moose (*Alces alces*) density, which in turn was controlled by wolf predation (McLaren & Peterson 1994). When the wolf population declined for any reason, moose reached high densities and suppressed fir growth. This top-down "trophic cascade" regulation is apparently replaced by bottom-up influences only when stand-replacing disturbances such as fire or large windstorms occur at times when moose density is already low (McLaren & Peterson 1994). This is strong evidence of top-down control of a food chain by wolves (Terborgh *et al.* 1999). Research elsewhere suggests elk (*Cervus elaphus*) populations not regulated by large predators affect negatively the growth of aspen (*Populus tremuloides*) (Kay 1990, Kay and Wagner 1994, White *et al.* 1992, D. Smith pers. comm.), though information remains equivocal (L. Morgantini pers. comm.).

In addition to the obvious interactions between wolves and prey, wolves provide a regular supply of carrion to scavengers. Less obvious community dynamics might include the relationships between different predators, and how wolves influence these relationships. For example, how do wolves modify the relationships between coyotes and foxes?

Interest in the role of wolves in the broader ecosystem is not new. From 1939-1944 Adolf Murie (1944) conducted field studies in Denali Park Alaska to determine "...the ecological picture centering about the wolf of Mount McKinley National Park". Here, he entertained questions about the relationships between park wolves and other wolves, between wolves and their prey, and between wolves and other predators. Few studies, however, are available to yield insights into many of the relationships between wolves and other ecosystem components.

e.   RESPONSE OF WOLVES TO HUMAN ACTIVITIES

The seriousness of human disturbance is ultimately a human judgement and, as such, some may consider any alteration of the normal activities of wolves to be undesirable. The ecological issue is how the probability of persistence changes with habitat degradation, small population size, and population isolation. The management issue is what probability of persistence and environmental quality is compatible with legislation and acceptable to society. Interpretation of the wolf-human interaction is confounded by multiple factors that influence how wolves use the landscape and react to people (Mladenoff *et al.* 1995, L. Boitani pers. comm., L. Carbyn pers. comm., E. Zimen pers. comm.). Because of the wolf's inherent behavioural variability, it is unlikely that all wolves react equally to human induced change. Moreover, many extraneous factors contribute to variance in behaviour of individual wolves. Because we have developed no reasonable expression of those differences, assessments are usually applied at the pack and population levels.

The specific conditions in which wolves are 'disturbed' (i.e., distribution, movements, survival, or fecundity are impaired) are believed to be highly variable. The extent and intensity of disturbance appear to vary with environmental and social context, and the individual animal (L. Boitani pers. comm.). Though wolves are sensitive to human predation and harassment (Thiel 1985, Jensen *et al.* 1986, Mech *et al.* 1988, Fuller 1989, Mech 1989, Purves *et al.* 1992, Fuller *et al.* 1992, Mech 1993, Mech 1995, Thurber *et al.* 1994, Mladenoff *et al.* 1995. Paquet *et al.* 1996), we have limited empirical information on tolerance to indirect human disturbance. Several studies suggest the main factor limiting wolves where they are present and tolerated by humans is adequate prey density (Fuller *et al.* 1992). Although human activities have been shown to influence the distribution (Thiel 1985, Fuller *et al.* 1992, Paquet 1993, Mladenoff *et al.* 1995) and survival of wolves (Mech *et al.* 1995, Mladenoff *et al.* 1995, Paquet 1993. Paquet *et al.* 1996), human-caused mortality is consistently cited as the major cause of displacement (Fuller *et al.* 1992, Mech and Goyal 1993, and others).

Studies that have quantified wolf/human interactions have shown wolves avoid humans or are displaced via human induced mortality (Paquet *et al.* 1996). Avoidance is temporal (Boitani 1982) and spatial (Mladenoff *et al.* 1995, Paquet *et al.* 1996). Several studies that used road densities as an index of human influence concluded that human activities associated with roads affect the survival and behaviour of wolves. Interpretation, however, was confounded because many human activities associated with roads result in the death of wolves. Thus, absence of wolves in an area may not be the result of behavioural avoidance per se. Data from Ontario, Wisconsin, Michigan, and Minnesota suggest that wolf survival is usually assured at road densities below 0.58 and 0.70 km/km² (Thiel 1985, Jensen *et al.* 1986, Mech *et al.* 1988, Fuller 1989, Mech 1989, Fuller *et al.* 1992). A study in Alaska concluded that wolves avoid heavily used roads and areas inhabited by humans, despite low human caused wolf mortality (Thurber *et al.* 1994). Landscape level analysis in Wisconsin found mean road density was much lower in pack territories (0.23 km/km² in 80% use area) than in random non pack areas (0.74) or the region overall (0.71). Few areas of use exceeded a road density of >0.45 km/km² (Mladenoff *et al.* 1995).

Recent reports suggest wolves in Minnesota tolerate higher levels of disturbance than previously thought possible. Wolves, for example, are now occupying ranges formerly assumed to be marginal because of prohibitive road densities and high human populations (Mech 1993, Mech 1995). Legal protection and changing human attitudes are cited as the critical factor in the wolf's ability to use areas that have not been wolf-habitat for decades. If wolves are not killed, they seem able to occupy areas of greater human activity than previously assumed (Mech 1993, Fuller *et al.* 1992). Based on these observations, Mech (1995, p. 275) comments that misconceptions about the wolf's inherent ability to tolerate human activity encourage unwarranted protection.

Nonetheless, wolves in Minnesota continue to avoid populated areas, occurring most often where road density and human population are low (Fuller *et al.* 1992).[2] Moreover, the fact that wolves are using areas of greater human activity suggests dispersers or marginalised individuals are being pushed into suboptimal habitat. More suitable and safe habitat may be saturated by dominant animals or packs. This supports the idea that wolves occupy habitat closer to humans only if necessary. A similar phenomenon has been shown in grizzly bears (D. Mattson *et al.* 1987, Mattson pers. Comm.) and many avian species.

We are aware of only 4 studies that have systematically and explicitly examined human population density and wolf distribution. In all studies, the absence of wolves in human dominated areas may have reflected high levels of human caused mortality, displacement resulting from behavioural avoidance, or some combination of both. All were conducted at a landscape scale and assessed population or pack level responses of wolves to humans. In Wisconsin, human population density was much lower in pack territories than in non pack areas. Wolf pack territories also had more public land, forested areas with at least some evergreens, and lower proportions of agricultural land. Notably, no difference was detected between white-tailed deer (*Odocoileus virginianus*) densities in pack territories and non pack areas. Overall, wolves selected those areas that were most remote from human influence (Mladenoff *et al.* 1995) using areas with fewer than 1.54 humans/km² and less than 0.15 km roads/km². Most wolves in Minnesota (88%) were in townships with <0.70 km roads/km² and <4 humans/km² or with <0.50 km² and <8 humans/km². High human or road densities likely precluded the presence of wolf packs in several localities within contiguous, occupied wolf range (Fuller *et al.* 1992). In Italy, wolf absence was related to human density, road density, urban areas, cultivated areas, and cattle and pig density. However, because human density, road density, and urbanized areas were highly inter correlated no specific human effect was established (Duprè *et al.* in press).

In the Bow River Valley, Alberta the selection or avoidance of particular habitat types was related to human use levels and habitat potential (Paquet *et al.* 1996). Wolves used disturbed habitats less than expected, which suggests the presence of humans altered their behaviour. Very low intensity disturbance (<100 people/month) did not have a significant influence on wolves, nor

---

[2]Wolves from the Midwestern United States have hybridized with coyotes (*Canis latrans*) (Wayne *et al.* 1991, Wayne *et al.* 1992, Lehman *et al.* 1991), or red wolf hybrids (Wilson *et al.* 2001), which may affect their behaviour (Fox 1971) and their relationship with humans. Consequently, extrapolating information from Minnesota, Michigan, Minnesota, and Ontario may be inappropriate for the Rocky Mountains. Wolves in the Rocky Mountains show no introgression of coyote genes (Forbes and Boyd 1996).

did it seriously affect the ecological relationships between wolves and their prey. At low to intermediate levels of human activity (100-1,000 people/month) wolves were dislocated from suboptimal habitats. Higher levels of activity resulted in partial displacement but not complete abandonment of preferred habitats. As disturbance increased, wolves avoided using some most favourable habitats. In portions of the Valley where high elk abundance was associated with high road and/or human population density, wolves were completely absent. Overall, habitat alienation resulted in altered predator/prey relationships.

The observed patterns of displacement suggest the presence of humans repulses wolves, although a strong attraction to highly preferred habitats increases a wolf's tolerance for disturbance. As conditions become less favorable, the quality of habitat likely takes on greater importance. Tolerance thresholds are unknown but, as noted, in the Bow River Valley changes in patterns of habitat use were evident when human activity exceeded 100 people/month. Nearly complete alienation of wolves occurred when more than 10,000 people/month used an area.

f.   HUMAN INFLUENCE ON HABITAT USE BY WOLVES

The degree of human influence probably varies according to the environmental context. If a particular habitat is highly attractive, wolves appear willing to risk exposure to humans, at least within some limits (Chapman 1977). As levels of disturbance increase, favorableness of habitat likely takes on greater importance. For example, we know that wolves select home sites near intense human activity when denning areas are limited, or where innocuous human activity occurs (Chapman 1977). The presence of artificial food sources (e.g., carrion pits, garbage dumps) also attracts wolves and reduces avoidance of human activity (Chapman 1977, L.D. Mech pers. comm., Paquet 1996, Krizan 1998). In the Bow River Valley, wolves denned within 500 m of the Trans Canada highway when Parks Canada was dumping carrion in the area. Wolves abandoned the home site after Parks stopped dumping of the carrion.

The tension between attraction and repulsion is probably expressed differently by individuals, packs, and populations. Attraction to an area is a complex sum of physiography, security from harassment, positive reinforcement (e.g., easily obtained food), population density, and available choice. Moreover, the response to a particular disturbance seems to depend on disturbance-history (E. Zimen pers. comm.); a critical concept in understanding the behaviour of long-lived animals that learn through social transmission (Curatolo and Murphy 1986, S. Minta pers. comm.).

We can group human influence into effects on wolf habitat and populations. Habitat disturbance can be short or long term and can include direct loss of habitat (i.e., vegetation removal, vegetation change, or isolation and removal of prey). Direct habitat loss does not include the loss of habitat due to temporal or spatial alienation (sensory disturbance) or from fragmentation of habitat. Indirect losses will occur due to habitat alienation, where wolves abandon habitat because of nearby disturbances or are spatially isolated from using them because of impediments to movements. Changes in population can occur directly through alterations in habitat and indirectly because of disturbing activities.

The major impacts of human induced changes are, in order of decreasing importance, physical loss of habitat, loss of prey species, fragmentation of habitat, isolation of habitat, alienation of habitat, alteration of habitat, changes in original ratios of habitat, and changes in juxtaposition of habitats. These effects combine to have local and population level influences by altering the composition of biological communities upon which wolves are dependent, restricting movements, reducing foraging opportunities, and limiting access to prey. Obstructing movements also increases the vulnerability of wolves to other disturbances as they attempt to learn new travel routes.

The degree to which human activities disrupt wildlife reflects the type and extent of disturbance, which interacts with the natural environment to affect environmental quality. In mountainous landscapes wildlife often responds markedly to disturbances that occur at small spatial scales. This is because the topography amplifies the effects of disturbances by concentrating activities of humans and wildlife into valley bottoms. The forced convergence of activities limits spatially the range of options wildlife have for coping with disruption, reducing resilience to anthropogenic disturbance (Weaver *et al.* 1996, Alaska Department of Fish and Game unpublished data).

Indirect human influences can affect an animal's chance to survive and reproduce. As wolves approach their limits of tolerance, they become increasingly susceptible to what would otherwise be minor influences. In the mountainous terrain, natural landforms and the condensed arrangement of habitats make wolves highly susceptible to the adverse effects of human disturbance. Because most development occurs in areas preferred by wolves, human activities unavoidably increase the risk of death and injury for wolves, decrease opportunities for wolves to move freely about, displace or alienates wolves from preferred ranges, and interrupt normal periods of activity. In less physiographically complex environments multiple travel routes link blocks of wolf habitat. Destruction or degradation of one or 2 routes is not usually critical, because safe alternative routes are available. In contrast, wolves living in mountains cannot avoid valley bottoms or use other travel routes without affecting their fitness. Therefore, tolerance of disturbance is probably lower than in other human dominated environments where wolves can avoid disturbed sites without seriously jeopardizing survival.

g.   RESPONSE OF WOLVES TO LINEAR DEVELOPMENTS

The security of wolf populations in the many regions may be tenuous, because linear developments heavily dissect wolf ranges (i.e., highways, secondary roads, railways, and power line corridors). Highway mortality has become a primary cause of wolf mortality and there is accumulating evidence of habitat loss, fragmentation, and degradation related to roads (Purves *et al.* 1992, Paquet 1993). Ensured connectivity of quality habitats is important for survival of large carnivores (Beier 1993, Paquet and Hackman 1995, Doak 1995, Noss *et al.* in press), especially for those that face a high risk of mortality from humans or vehicles when travelling across settled landscapes (Noss 1992, Beier 1993).

There are several plausible explanations for the absence of wolves in densely roaded areas. Wolves may behaviourally avoid densely roaded areas depending on the type of use the road receives (Thurber *et al.* 1994). In other instances, their absence may be a direct result of mortality associated with roads (Van Ballenberhe *et al.* 1975, Mech 1977, Berg and Kuehn 1982). Besides fragmenting and consuming critical habitat, linear developments provide access to remote regions, which allows humans to deliberately, accidentally, or incidentally kill wolves (Van Ballenberghe *et al.* 1975, Mech 1977, Berg and Kuehn 1982). Despite legal protection, 80% of known wolf mortality in a Minnesota study was human-caused (30% shot, 12% snared, 11% hit by vehicles, 6% killed by government trappers, and 21% killed by humans in some undetermined manner) (Fuller 1989). Mech (1989) reported 60% of human-caused mortality in a roaded area (even after full protection), whereas human caused mortality was absent in an adjoining region without roads. On the east side of the Central Rockies between 1986 and 1993, human caused mortality was 95% of known wolf death. Thirty-six percent (36%) of mortality was related to roads (Paquet 1993).

Wolves also experience higher mortality in areas with higher road density. On Prince of Wales Island, Alaska, researchers report a significant jump in wolf mortality (kill/259 km²) in areas where road densities exceeds.25 km/km². While wolf mortality in the category of most densely roaded areas is highest, the variance is also high. The authors suggest that at some threshold of road density or human activity, wolves may abandon an area, resulting in decreased trapping and hunting mortality (Alaska Department of Fish and Game, unpublished data).

Linear developments may also be physical and/or psychological impediments to wolf movement. Road density and human density have been inversely correlated with viable populations of wolves in several areas. Along the Ontario-Michigan border, distribution of breeding packs occurred only in Ontario. Except for Cockburn Island, only lone wolves were found in areas close to the border or in Michigan. In Ontario, the density of roads in areas not occupied by wolves was greater than in areas occupied by wolves. Mean road density in Michigan, where no wolves resided, was also greater than in wolf-occupied areas of Ontario. High human densities, represented by road densities of > 0.6 km/km², were believed to be a barrier to wolf dispersal into Michigan (Jensen *et al.* 1986).

Studies in Wisconsin, Michigan, Ontario, and Minnesota have shown a strong relationship between road density and the absence of wolves (Thiel 1985, Jensen *et al.* 1986, Mech *et al.* 1988, Fuller 1989). Wolves generally are not present where the density of roads exceeds 0.58 km/km² (Thiel 1985 and Jensen *et al.* 1986, cf. Fuller 1989). Landscape level analysis in Wisconsin, Minnesota, and Michigan found mean road density was much lower in pack territories (0.23 km/km² in 80% use area) than in random nonpack areas (0.74) or the region overall (0.71). Road density was the strongest predictor of wolf habitat favorability out of 5 habitat characteristics and 6 indices of landscape complexity (Mladenoff *et al.* 1995). Few areas of use exceeded a road density of >0.45 km/km² (Mladenoff *et al.* 1995). Notably, radio collared packs were not bisected by any major federal or state highway. In Minnesota, densities of roads for the primary range, peripheral range, and disjunct range of wolves were all below a threshold of 0.58 km/km². These results, however, probably do not apply to areas on which public access is restricted. Mech (1989), for example, reported wolves using an area with a road density of 0.76 km/km², but it was next to a large, roadless area. He speculated that excessive mortality experienced by wolves in the roaded area was compensated for by individuals that dispersed from the adjacent roadless area. Wolves on Prince of Wales Island, Alaska currently use areas with road densities greater than 0.58 km/km². Core areas, however, are generally in the least densely roaded areas of the home range, and wolf activity that does occur in densely roaded areas occurs primarily at night. This behavioral response may reflect the limited options wolves have to relocate when they live on islands or insularized landscapes.

The response of wolves to different road types and human presence at the boundaries of Kenai National Wildlife Refuge, Alaska, was examined in a study of radio-collared wolves (Thurber *et al.* 1994). Wolves avoided oilfield access roads open to public use, yet were attracted to a gated pipeline access road and secondary gravel roads with limited human use. Thurber *et al.* speculated that roads with low human activity provide easy travel corridors for wolves. The response of wolves to a major public highway was equivocal. They thought wolf absence from settled areas and some roads were caused by behavioral avoidance rather than direct attrition resulting from killing of animals. In Montana, Singleton (1995) found that wolves preferred areas 0.5-1 km from open roads for travel routes. He speculated that wolves did not select locations more distant from open roads because of the distribution patterns of wintering ungulates and the barrier provided by the river. Overall, wolves preferred areas with 0.01-2 mi/mi² for travel routes.

5. HAVE WOLVES SUCCESSFULLY ESTABLISHED HOME RANGES WITHIN THE DESIGNATED WOLF RECOVERY AREA?

a. BACKGROUND

Biologists usually define the home range of a wolf as an area within which it can meet all of its annual biological requirements. Seasonal feeding habitat, thermal and security needs, travel, denning, the bearing and raising of young, are all essential life requirements. The manner in which habitats for these requirements are used and distributed influences home range size and local and regional population distributions. Generally, wolves locate their home ranges in areas where adequate prey are available and human disturbance minimal (Mladenoff *et al*. 1995, 1997, Mladenoff and Sickley 1998). Wolves use areas within those home ranges in ways that maximize encounters with prey (Huggard 1993a, b).

Newly colonizing wolf pack might shift home ranges in response to climate, food availability, human disturbance, and other factors. A colonizing pack might have a larger, more fluid, home range than a pack surrounded by other wolf packs (Boyd *et al*. 1996). Some evidence suggests that wolf packs colonize areas that were first "pioneered" by dispersing lone wolves (Ream *et al*. 1991)

In mountainous areas, topographic position influences selection of home ranges and travel routes (Paquet *et al*. 1996). Wolf use of valley bottoms and lower slopes correspond to the presence of wintering ungulate prey and snow depth in these areas (Singer 1979, Jenkins and Wright 1988, Paquet *et al*. 1996). In areas of higher prey density pack sizes increase (Messier 1985) and home range size is closely correlated with pack size (Messier 1985, Peterson *et al*. 1984).

b. DATA SUMMARY

We assessed home ranges using locations from radio-collared animals. Radio-telemetry data (>7000 locations) were provided in an Excel database (Monitor). These data include all telemetry locations from 3 March 1998 to 3 March 2001. Each location was appended by wolf identification, date, time, and pack membership. Although locations were qualitatively ranked for accuracy, no quantitative assessment of telemetry error was available. Thus, we classified locations into 4 categories, which corresponded to the database provided. Class 1, 2, 3, and 4 locations were those within 100 m, 100-250 m, 250-450 m, and greater than 450 m from the true location, respectively. Only class 1 aerial and ground locations were used in the home range analysis.

c. METHODS

Our objective was to quantitatively describe areal distribution of reintroduced Mexican wolves within the recovery region. In a few cases, however, subjective determination of the home range was more appropriate.

Using ArcView Spatial Analyst, we plotted all class 1 locations. We discarded locations deemed to be recording errors, extraterritorial forays, and dispersals. We assumed a wolf dispersed if it permanently left its original pack and formed a new pack or joined an existing one (Messier 1985b).

Locations of individual wolves were grouped by pack affiliation. We defined a pack as 2 or more wolves that traveled together more than 1 month (Messier 1984). For each pack we used one wolf/year to represent the annual home range of the pack. This is a reasonable assumption if a high degree of association exists between pack members (Kolenosky and Johnston 1967, Fuller and Keith 1980, Fritts and Mech 1981, Ciucci *et al.* 1997). We confirmed pack affiliations by examining telemetry locations of wolves believed to be associating and through visual observations of the wolves by the field crew.

We used Home Range and Ranges V® software (Kenward and Hodder 1996) to calculate annual (1 Apr–31 Mar) and seasonal 95% minimum convex polygons (Mohr 1947) for individual packs and the entire free ranging wolf population within the primary zone and recovery area (Apache/Gila N.F.). Home range is an extension of ArcView Spatial Analyst. We assumed home ranges were defined when the observation-area curve formed an asymptote (Kenward and Hodder 1996) and locations were obtained throughout the year.

Accuracy of aerial and ground locations for the entire study was estimated to be 250 m, which is the highest mean error of telemetry obtained by researchers on other wolf projects. To account for the 250-m error, we changed the fix resolution from the RangesV® software default of 1 m to 250 m. This resolution is used to set the width of the boundary strip that is included in polygon edges and areas (Kenward and Hodder 1996, R. Kenward, pers. comm.). We left the scaling parameter at the software default of 1 m, which means that each coordinate unit was 1 m from the next.

d.   RESULTS

From 1998 through 2001, 9 wolf packs were identified by name in the telemetry database. However, the criteria for specifying packs were not always biological. Release sites, geographic locations, and affiliations with other wolves influenced pack designation. Packs, pack compositions, and configurations of home ranges changed as reintroduced wolves encountered other wolves, and established new territories. In addition, the frequent removal and reintroduction of wolves confounded the assignment of individual wolves to specific packs.

The number of recorded aerial and ground locations varied among wolf packs (Figure 1). For the most part, the frequency of locations reflected the time that radio collared wolves were free-ranging, rather than differential effort by the field crew. Time of year, however, affected the number of locations acquired (Figure 2). Discussions with the field team confirmed that for logistic reasons they reduced monitoring activities in winter. We identified some locations that were far outside the reintroduction area. Many of these were recording or data entry errors (Figure 3). Several, however, were from wandering or dispersing wolves.

The proportion of telemetry locations within the primary recovery zone (Apache N.F.) and within the Blue Range wolf recovery area (Apache/Gila N.F.) varied among packs (Figure 4). Temporal trends in the proportion of telemetry locations (pooled across all packs) within the primary zone and within the recovery area also varied (Figure 5). The approximate area occupied by free-ranging Mexican wolf population changed over time as did the density of wolves. This was partially a reflection of periodic releases and recaptures of wolves, and also free-ranging wolves shifting centers of activity as they established pack affiliations and home ranges (Figures 6, 7, 8).

Many individuals and packs showed home range fidelity typical of wolves with established territories (Figure 9). However, frequent social disruption via mortality, recaptures, and re-releases may have altered the natural territorial behavior of packs. Wolves are long-lived social carnivores that transmit information between generations and among individual pack members. In this regard, the establishment, location, and maintenance of home ranges likely depend on a stable pack structure and the persistence of traditional pack knowledge. The home range behavior of reintroduced wolves may be highly susceptible to social disruption because they lack a cognitive map of the area. Moreover, lack of familiarity with the landscape may have a stronger influence on captive reared animals than wild born.

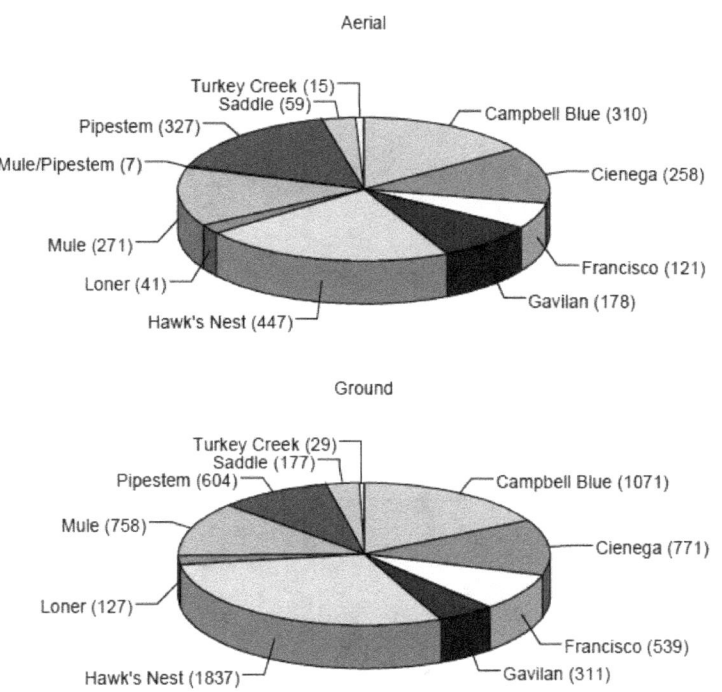

Figure 1. Summary of Mexican wolf radio telemetry data, 1998-2001. Numbers in parentheses are telemetry locations recorded.

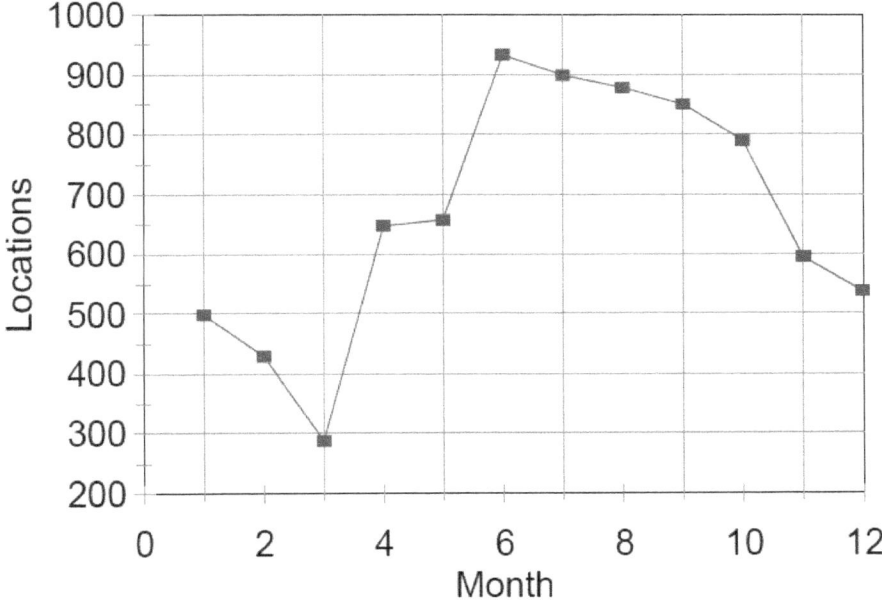

Figure 2. Monthly radio-telemetry locations of reintroduced Mexican wolves, Arizona, 1998-2001.

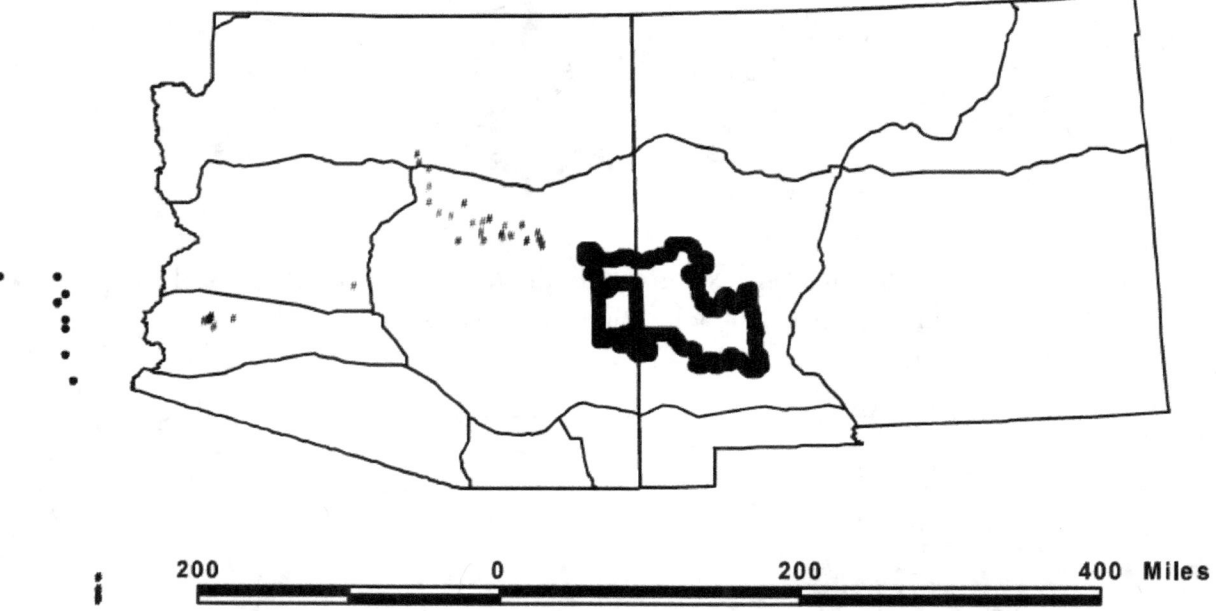

Figure 3. Many telemetry locations resulted from data entry errors. For example, numerous locations were in the state of California and in the Gulf of California.

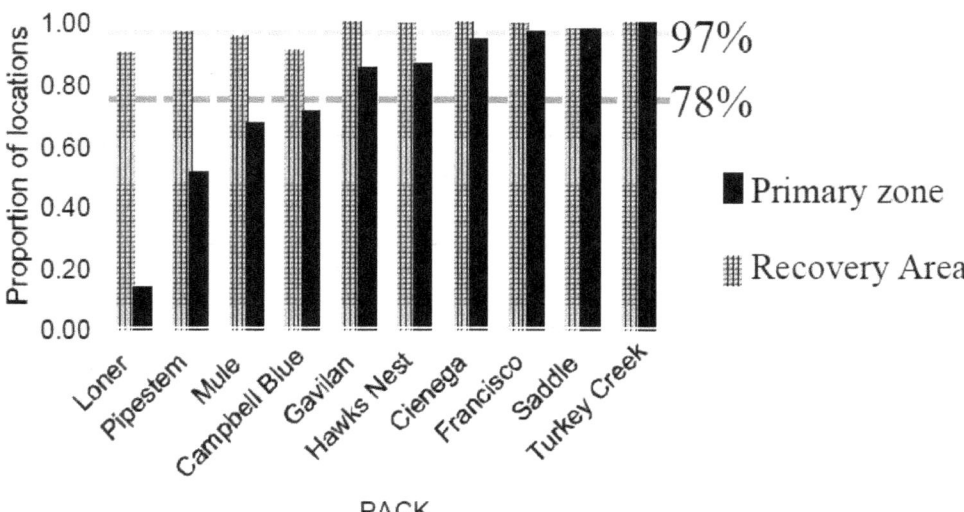

Figure 4. Variation among wolf packs in the proportion of telemetry locations within the primary zone and within the recovery area (Apache/Gila N.F.). These data include all telemetry locations of reintroduced Mexican wolves from 3 March 1998 to 3 March 2001.

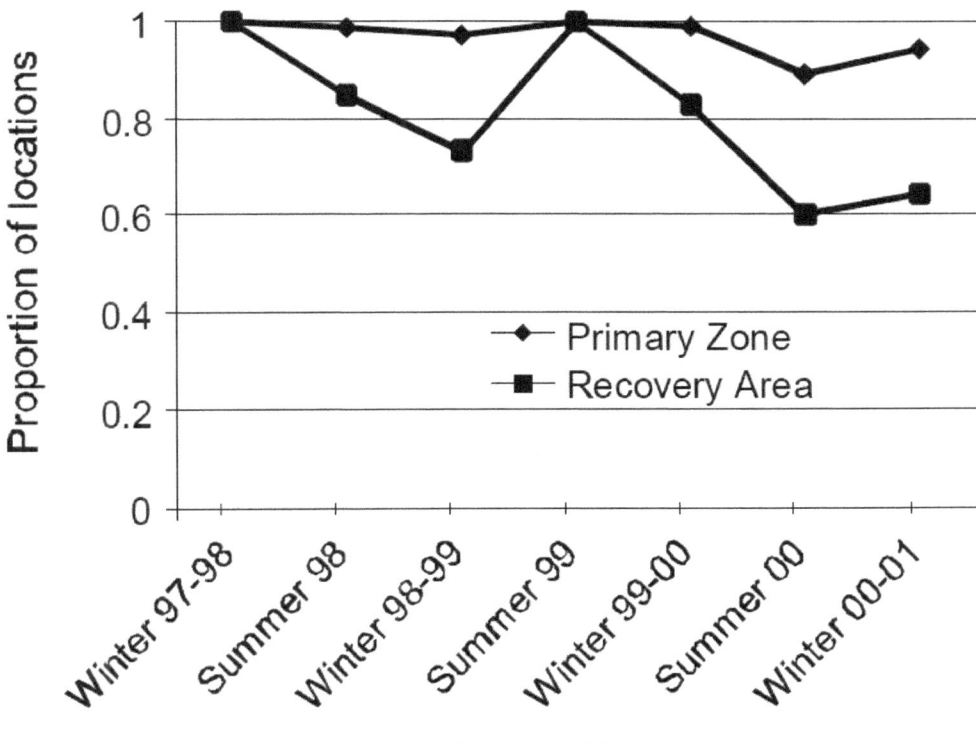

Figure 5. Temporal trends in the proportion of telemetry locations (pooled across all packs) within the primary zone (Apache N.F.) and within the recovery area (Apache/Gila N.F.). These data include all telemetry locations of reintroduced Mexican wolves from 3 March 1998 to 3 March 2001.

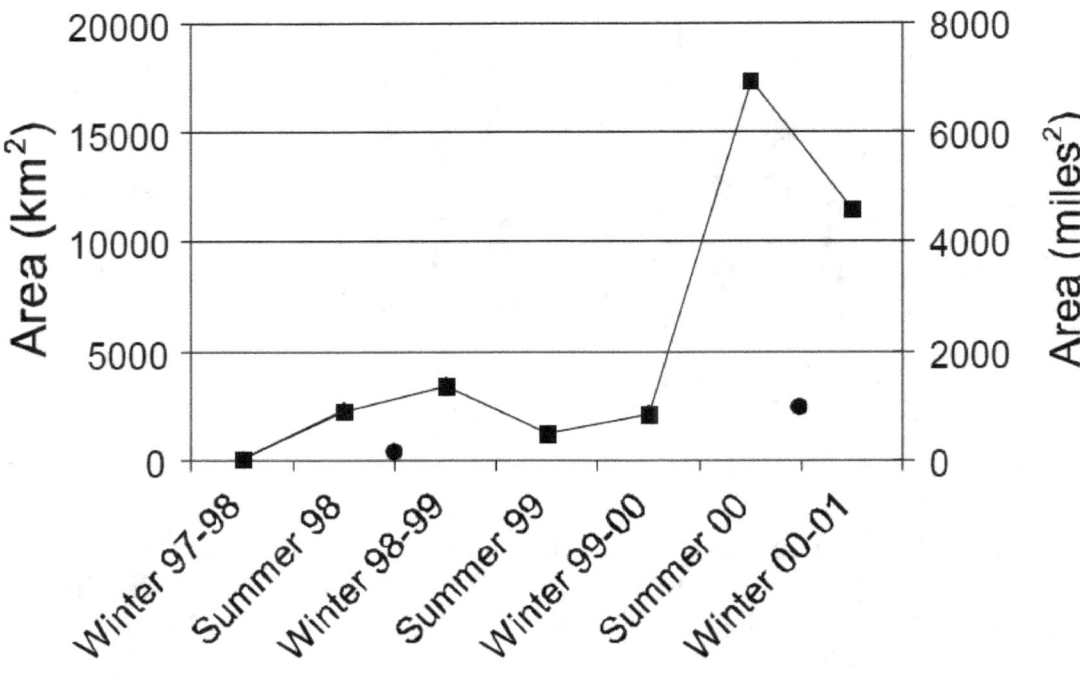

Figure 6. Approximate area occupied by free- ranging Mexican wolf population in Arizona and New Mexico, 1998-2001.

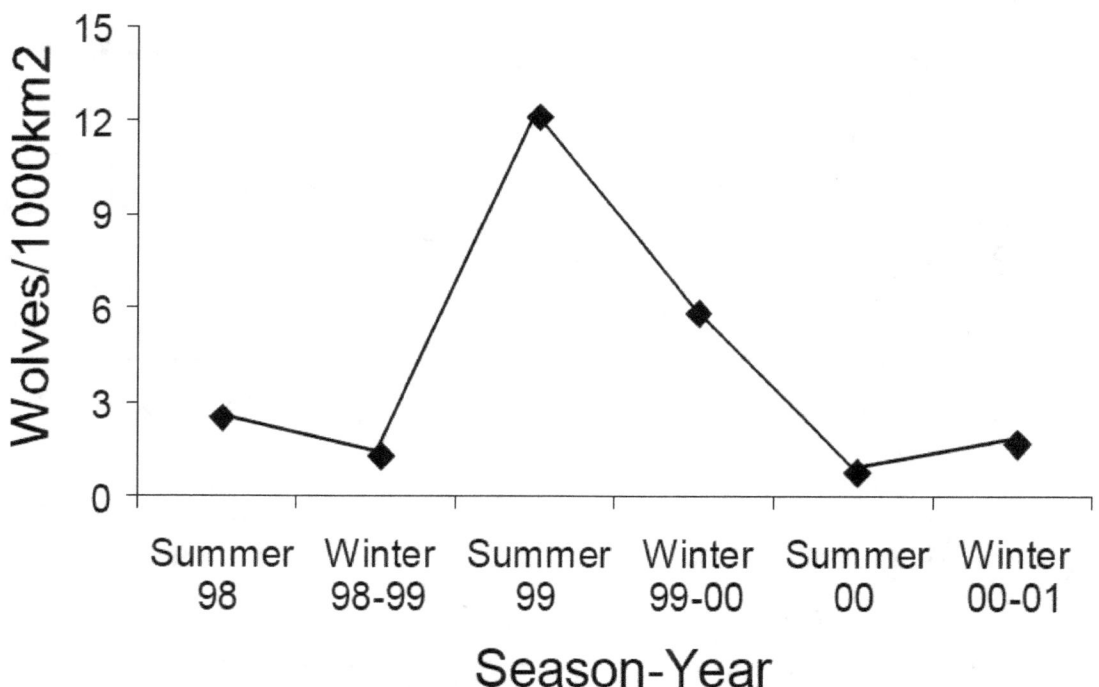

Figure 7. Density of free-ranging Mexican wolf population in Arizona and New Mexico, 1998-2001.

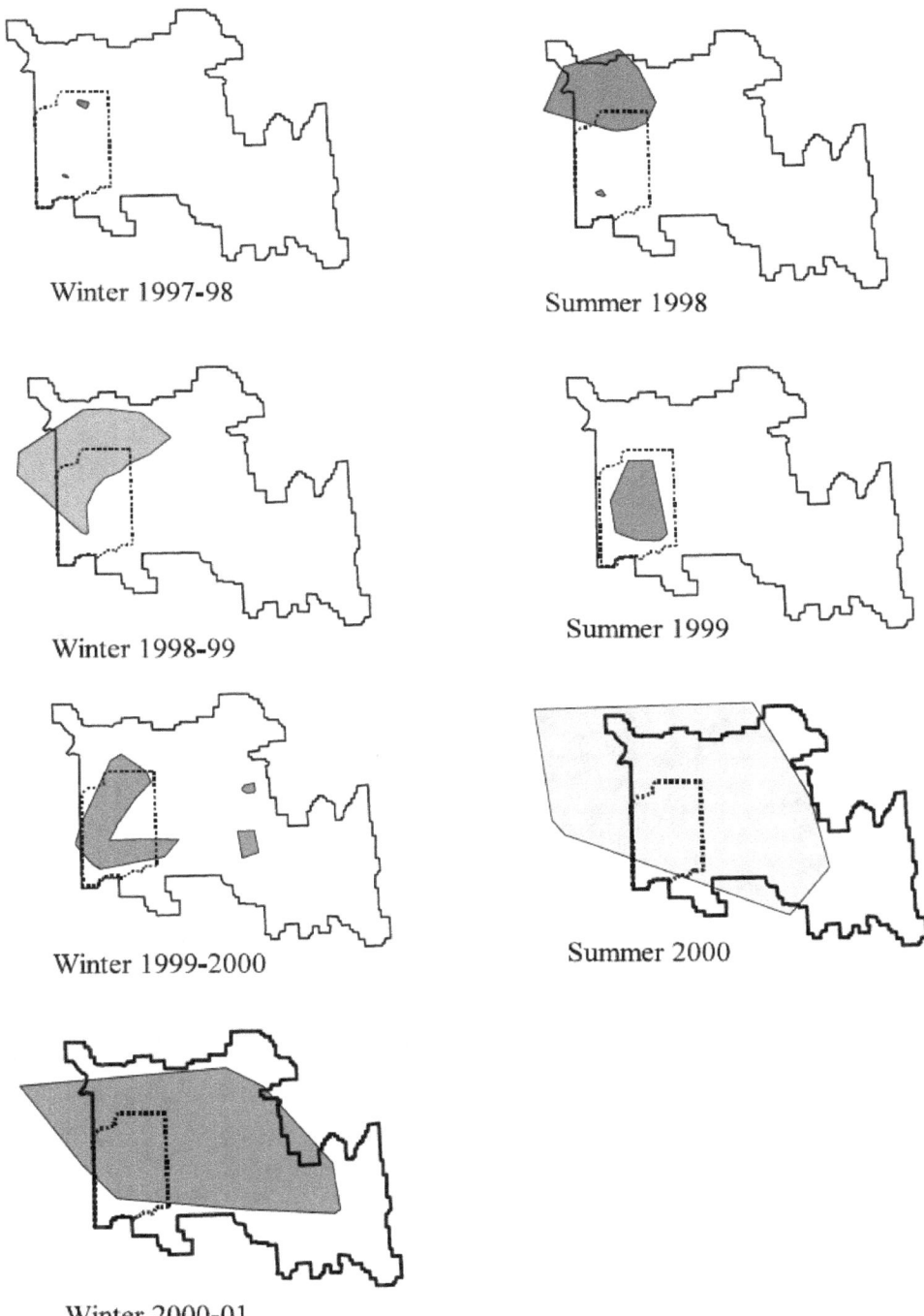

Winter 1997-98

Summer 1998

Winter 1998-99

Summer 1999

Winter 1999-2000

Summer 2000

Winter 2000-01

Figure 8. Seasonal distribution of free-ranging Mexican wolf population in Arizona and New Mexico, 1998-2001.

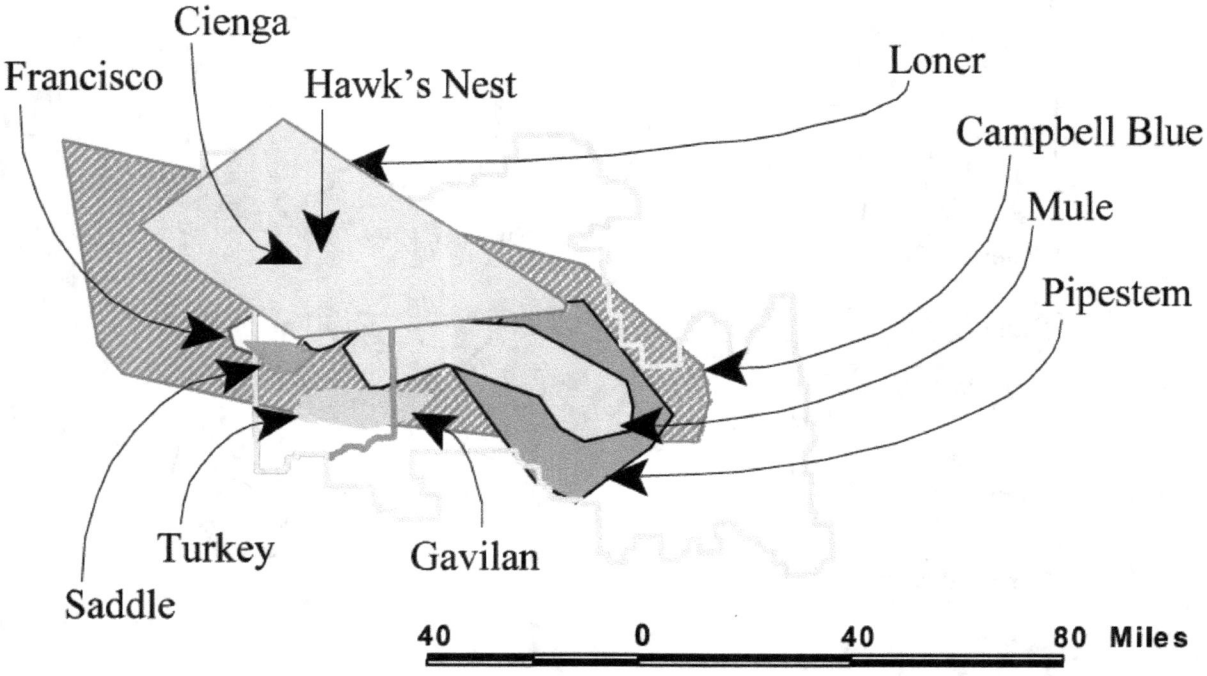

Figure 9. Polygons reflecting the spatial extent of pack home ranges in relation to the primary zone (Apache N.F.) And recovery area (Apache/Gila N.F.). These data include all telemetry locations of reintroduced Mexican wolves from 03 March 1998 to 03 March 2001.

e.   CONCLUSIONS

We conclude that some wolves have successfully established home ranges and possibly pack territories within the designated wolf recovery area. We caution, however, that frequent recaptures and re-releases confounded our analysis. These manipulations may also be interfering with pack formation and establishment and maintenance of home ranges. Lastly, individual wolves have shown some indication of dispersing outside the recovery area. This is to be expected and required if the regional population is to be viable.

6.　HAVE REINTRODUCED WOLVES REPRODUCED SUCCESSFULLY IN THE WILD?

　　a.　BACKGROUND
　　　　i.　Births versus recruitment
　　　　　　(1)　Compared with adults, pups have relatively low survival rates during the first year of life.
　　　　　　(2)　In a sense, pups do not really contribute to the viability of a population until they have survived a period of high mortality rate associated with being a pup.
　　　　　　(3)　Although the EIS refers to projected numbers of pups, the projections seem to treat pups as though they have been recruited into the adult population (i.e., with survival rates like adults).

　　b.　DATA SUMMARY

We used information recorded in the telemetry and events databases. Additional information on reproduction was garnered from discussions with the Field Team. Dense vegetation and the secretive nature of wolves precluded regular and accurate visuals of wolves. Consequently, the Interagency Field Team did not routinely observe wolves during spring and summer when pups are easiest to distinguish from adults. We assumed the presence of dens and rendezvous sites when movements became localized in April through July or when lactating females or pups were captured. Sometimes, ground checks confirmed potential denning and rendezvous areas.

　　c.　METHODS

We determined natality directly from field observations of dens, rendezvous sites (pup rearing and resting areas), and packs. We ascertained successful year-specific reproduction using changes in pack size from March to the following December. We assumed unsuccessful reproduction (i.e., no or failed reproduction) when a pack did not display focal activities in the summer. Annual recruitment was derived from winter pack sizes recorded in February.

　　d.　RESULTS

Births have taken place in the wild (Table 1). Births and recruitment rates, however are lower than projected in the EIS (Figures 10 and 11).

Table 1. Known births and recruitments of reintroduced Mexican wolves recorded from 1998-2001. Only 1 litter was conceived in the wild.

PARENTS				
Female	Male	ESTIMATED DATE OF BIRTH (M/D/Y)	CONCEIVED IN WILD?	WILD BIRTHS
174	166	35915	No	Litter of 5 pups (known number due to necropsy report showing 5 placental scars); one survived to ~ 4 months., then disappeared after 174 was killed.
191	208	5/1/99	No	Litter of unknown number (6 confirmed).
482	166	5/1/99	No	Litter of 6 pups (known number due to necropsy report showing 6 placental scars); pups were never documented for this pair by the field team --pair never settled in an area so likely pups were lost immediately.
486	131	5/1/00	Yes	Litter of unknown number (one confirmed).
191	208	5/1/00	No	Litter of unknown number (one confirmed).
189	190	4/15/00	No	Litter of unknown number

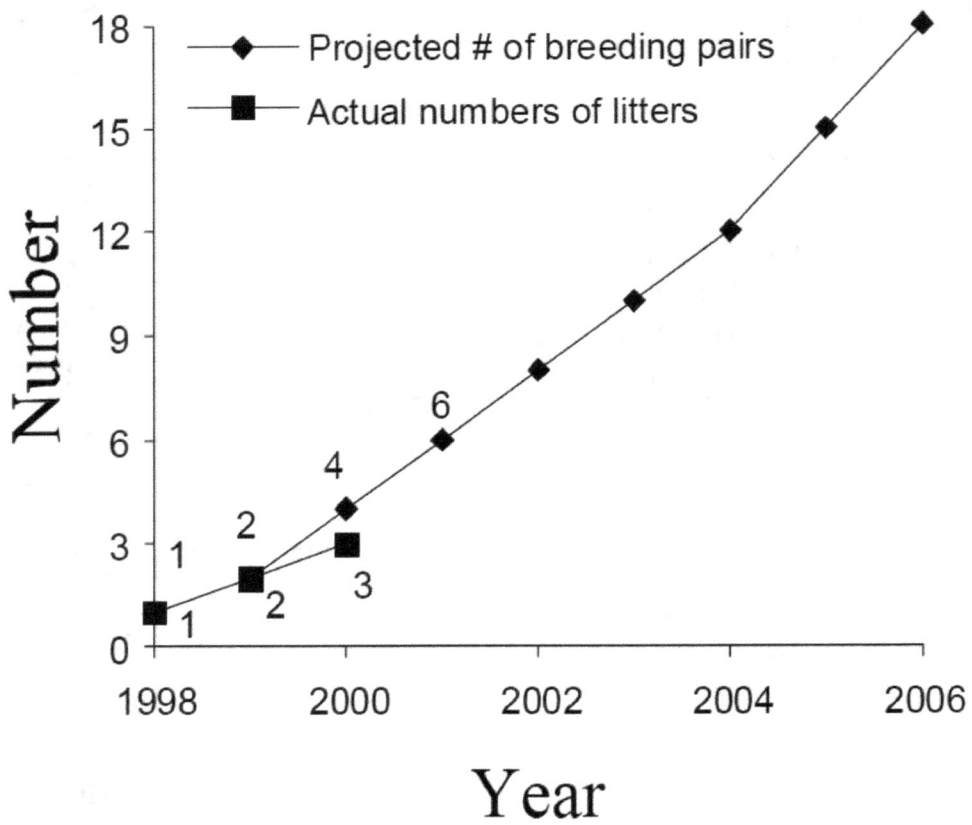

Figure 10. Projected numbers of breeding pairs (in the EIS) and actual numbers of litters for reintroduced Mexican wolves, 1998-2001.

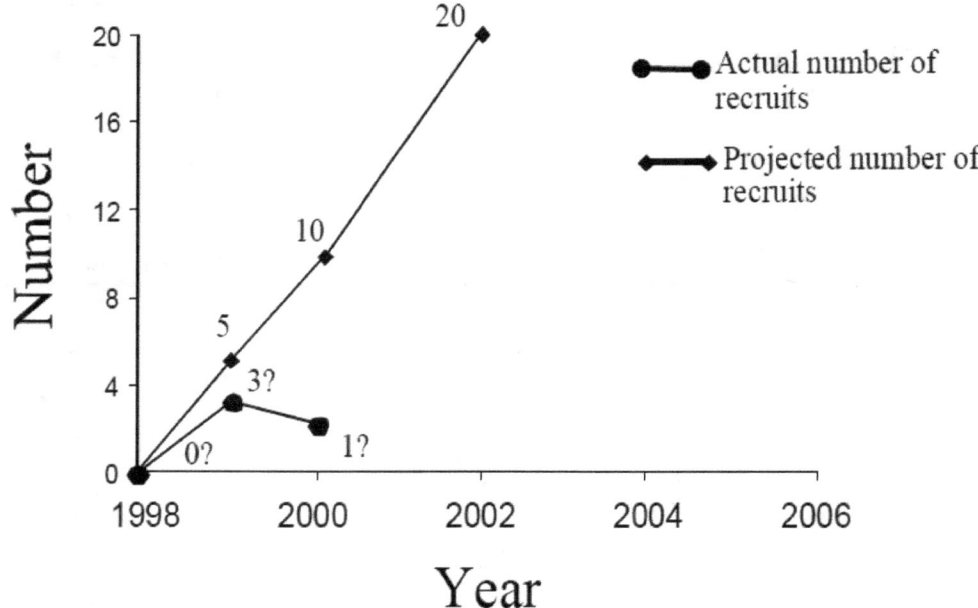

Figure 11. Actual and projected numbers of recruits for reintroduced Mexican wolves, 1998-2001.

e.   CONCLUSIONS

The number of free-ranging Mexican wolves at the end of third year is similar to that projected in the EIS. Survival and recruitment rates, however are far too low to ensure population growth or persistence. Without dramatic improvement in theses vital rates, the wolf population will fall short of predictions for upcoming years.

7.   IS WOLF MORTALITY SUBSTANTIALLY HIGHER THAN PROJECTED IN THE EIS?

a.   BACKGROUND

Researchers do not agree on the annual rate of mortality that causes a population decline in wolves. However, Keith (1983) and Fuller (1989) reviewed several wolf studies across North America and concluded that harvests exceeding 28-30% of fall populations resulted in declines. Fuller (1989) further concluded that populations would stabilize with an overall annual mortality rate of 35%. He felt, however, the effects of harvest could vary with time and population structure. Specifically, a population containing many pups could withstand much higher mortality.

Various researchers have suggested different rates of annual mortality they believe control growth of wolf populations. However, the annual rate of mortality that causes a population decline in wolves is unknown. Furthermore, many researchers consider only harvest (hunting or trapping) when they calculate mortality rates that cause wolf population declines. For instance Mech (1970) concluded an annual harvest of 50% or more was necessary to control wolf populations based on pup-adult ratios but did not distinguish between harvest and natural mortality. Keith (1983) reviewed studies of 13 exploited populations and determined that harvests exceeding 30% of fall populations resulted in population declines. Similarly Fuller (1989) found annual rates of wolf increase vary in direct response to rates of mortality and where humans kill wolves, harvests exceeding 28% of autumn or early winter populations might result in a population decline. He concluded a population would stabilize with an overall rate of annual mortality of 0.35 or rate of human-caused mortality of 0.28. Consequently, the exact relationship between the annual rate of mortality from all human causes (harvest, collisions with cars and trains) and population limitation or decline in wolves is uncertain.

In areas where ungulate biomass is low, researchers have noted that starvation and intraspecific aggression are common. For instance, in southwestern Quebec, Messier (1985a) noted wolves with fewer prey available incurred more deaths from natural causes, namely starvation and intraspecific aggression. Similarly, Mech (1977a) noted occurrence of starvation and intraspecific aggression increased as prey availability declined in Minnesota. Disease cannot be linked with certainty to low availability of food but the relationship makes sense intuitively. A population of wolves lacking food should be more vulnerable to disease than one with more food available. Furthermore, food shortage leading to nutritional stress could combine with disease factors to increase the significance of otherwise innocuous or sub-lethal conditions (Brand *et al.* 1995).

In most studies, no disease-related mortality has been reported (VanBallenberghe *et al.* 1975, Mech 1977a, Fritts and Mech 1981, Messier 1985a, Potvin 1987, Ballard *et al.* 1989, Hayes *et al.* 1991, Meier *et al.* 1995, Pletscher *et al.* 1997). In other studies, from 2-21% of wolf mortality has been attributed to disease (Carbyn 1982, Peterson *et al.* 1984, Fuller 1989, Ballard *et al.* 1997). Ballard *et al.* (1997) concluded that occurrence of rabies was a significant factor in a decline of wolves from Alaska. In that study, rabies-caused mortality was 21%.

Quantifying the importance of food in limiting population growth based on cause of death alone is difficult. In the literature, results vary among studies. On Isle Royale, annual mortality from starvation and intraspecific strife (both related to low food availability) ranged from 18-57% during a 20-year period (Peterson and Page 1988). In populations where some human-caused mortality occurs, and thus compensates for natural mortality (starvation, accidents, disease and intraspecific strife), about 8% of individuals greater than 6 months-of-age can be lost each year (Ballard *et al.* 1987, Fuller 1989). Some researchers have accepted this variability and decided any sign of starvation among adult wolves means food is limiting population growth (Fritts and Mech 1981, Ballard *et al.* 1997, P. Paquet, pers. comm.). This assumption is reasonable given adults typically are the last members of the population affected by food shortage (Eberhardt 1977) and as such, may be the most sensitive indicators of a shortage of food.

Human-caused mortality can also be an important limiting factor (Peterson *et al.* 1984; Ballard *et al.* 1989, 1997). However, quantifying the importance of human-caused mortality as a limiting factor is difficult. These causes include legal harvest (Fuller and Keith 1980, Keith 1983, Gasaway *et al.* 1983, Messier 1985a, Ballard *et al.* 1987, 1997, Peterson *et al.* 1984, Potvin 1987, Bjorge and Gunson 1989, Fuller 1989, Hayes *et al.* 1991, Pletscher *et al.* 1997), illegal harvest (Fritts and Mech 1981, Fuller 1989, Pletscher *et al.* 1997), vehicles on highways (Berg and Kuehn 1982, Potvin 1987, Fuller 1989, Paquet 1993, Parks Canada 1994, Forbes and Theberge 1995, Paquet and Hackman 1995, Thiel and Valen 1995, Bangs and Fritts 1996), and trains (Paquet 1993, Parks Canada 1994, Paquet and Hackman 1995, Paquet *et al.* 1996).

b.   DATA SUMMARY

We used information recorded in the telemetry and events databases. Additional information, clarification of events, and interpretation of events was provided by the Interagency Field Team. All free-ranging Mexican wolves were radio-collared from time of release. Moreover, each radio-collared Mexican wolf was and continues to be relocated regularly and frequently via ground and aerial telemetry. Frequent monitoring reveals whether each wolf is alive or dead at the time of relocation

c.   METHODS

We were not able to address the question of annual mortality directly because removals and re-releases precluded calculating annual rates of mortality. Thus, we estimated survival rates for the Mexican wolf population and then compared these estimated values with the survival rates projected in the EIS. Survival rate is the chance (or probability) of surviving some specified time. Survival rates are typically expressed as values between zero and one. For example, if the annual survival rate of an individual is 0.82, we would say that individual has an 82% chance of surviving during the next year. Survival is a critical population process and estimating survival rates is an important part of measuring viability of populations. Management of protected wolf populations requires quantitative survival measurements to identify factors that drive population change. From the survival rate one can also understand the mortality rate. The mortality rate of an individual or population is one minus the survival rate.

Using the telemetry data we compiled a table showing the number of wolves that were alive each month, died each month, and recaptured each month. The table provided the foundation for formal analysis of survival rates. We estimated survival rates of radio-collared wolves using the Kaplan-Meier (K-M) product limit estimator (Kaplan EL and Meier 1958). We carried out this analysis using the programs MARK and Minitab (Version 12). Conceptually, the analysis uses the relationships between the number of wolves that die each month and the number monitored each month. Although estimating a rate of survival for each month is possible, the data show that annual survival rates do not vary substantially across longer periods. Thus, we estimated survival rates using an information-theoretic approach (Buhrnam and Anderson 1999) that determines the most appropriate time scale (e.g., monthly, seasonally, or annually).

From the perspective of a free-ranging population, returning a wolf to captivity (from now on, recapture event) is equivalent to a mortality event. Thus, we conducted 2 survival analyses. One analysis considered only true biological deaths, and the other treated biological deaths and recapture events as mortality events. In both analyses, we reincluded wolves from time of release until "mortality" or disappearance of the radio-signal occurred.

Sample sizes were too small to use Cox's proportional hazards model and determine the influence of important covariates (such as age and sex) on survival. We did not calculate cause-specific mortality. Mortality was described, however, using percents. We assumed that the proximate cause of death was the ultimate cause of death. We were unable to assess the relative importance of other factors that may have been involved.

The starting date of the survival study was March 1998 and the end date was March 2001. For known deaths we estimated the date of mortality to the nearest day using evidence from the telemetry and events data bases. When information was unavailable, we deemed day of mortality the midpoint of the interval between the last day the wolf was known alive and the day it was discovered dead. The cause of mortality was often identified on site and when possible, confirmed by necropsy (Interagency Field Team pers. comm.)

d.　　RESULTS

Forty-seven (47) wolves were monitored From March 1998 (when Mexican wolves were first released) to March 2001. Twenty-three (23) wolves are currently being monitored. Four (4) wolves are unaccounted for. Twenty (20) wolves were recaptured following release. Nine (9) of these were re-released and are known to be alive. Two (2) wolves were re-released but contact was lost and their fate is unknown. One of the re-released wolves died. Eight (8) of the recaptured wolves were not re-released and some died in captivity. Seventeen (17) wolves are known to have died, 10 in the wild (Figure 12). Human caused mortality was the most common cause of death. Of the human related deaths, most were caused by gunshots (Figure 13). Wolves also died from distemper and parvovirus. Both these diseases are contracted or originally spread from domestic animals. Death by disease was higher than projected in the EIS.

When recaptures were included as mortalities, survival rates were lower than projected in the EIS (Figure 14). Excluding recaptures as mortalities resulted in survival rates exceeding the EIS projections in 1999 and 2000 (Figure 15). Survival rates from either method, however, were lower than for wolves in the Flathead region of Montana and British Columbia (Pletscher *et al.* 1997), lower than for wolves in the central Canadian Rocky Mountains, lower than a recovering wolf population in the Yukon (Hayes and Harestad 2000), and higher than an exploited population in Alaska (Ballard *et al.* 1987).

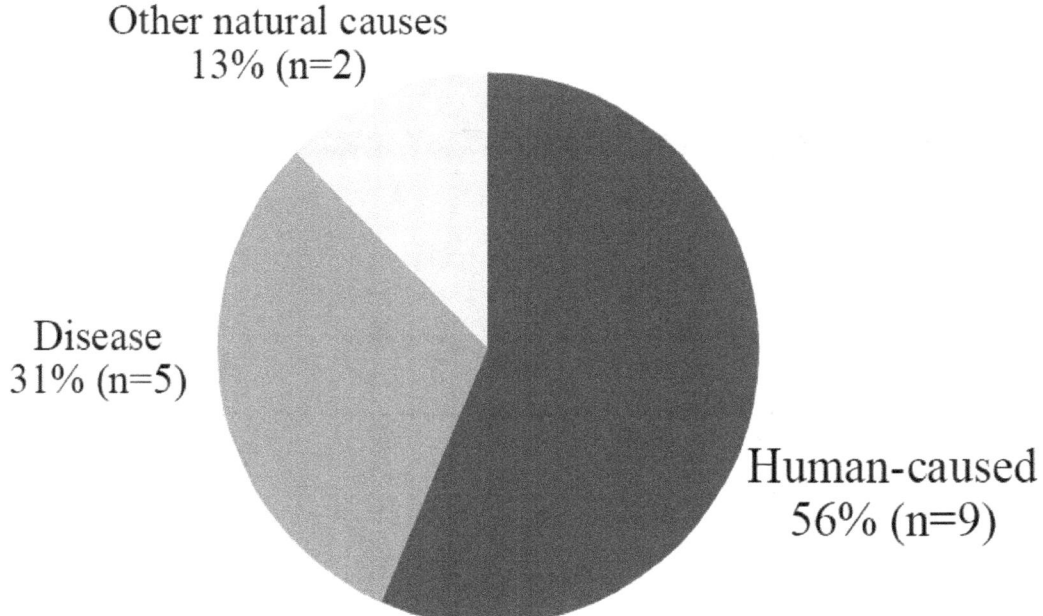

Figure 12. Causes of wolf mortality for Mexican wolves reintroduced to Arizona, 1998-2001.

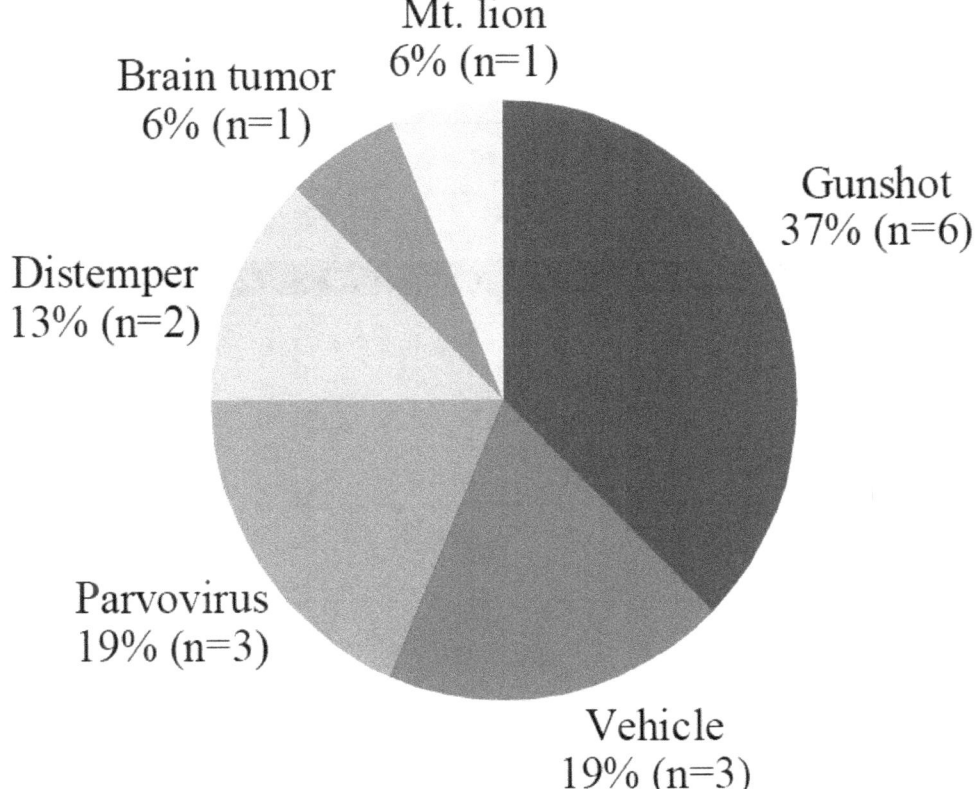

Figure 13. Cause specific wolf mortality for Mexican wolves reintroduced to Arizona, 1998-2001.

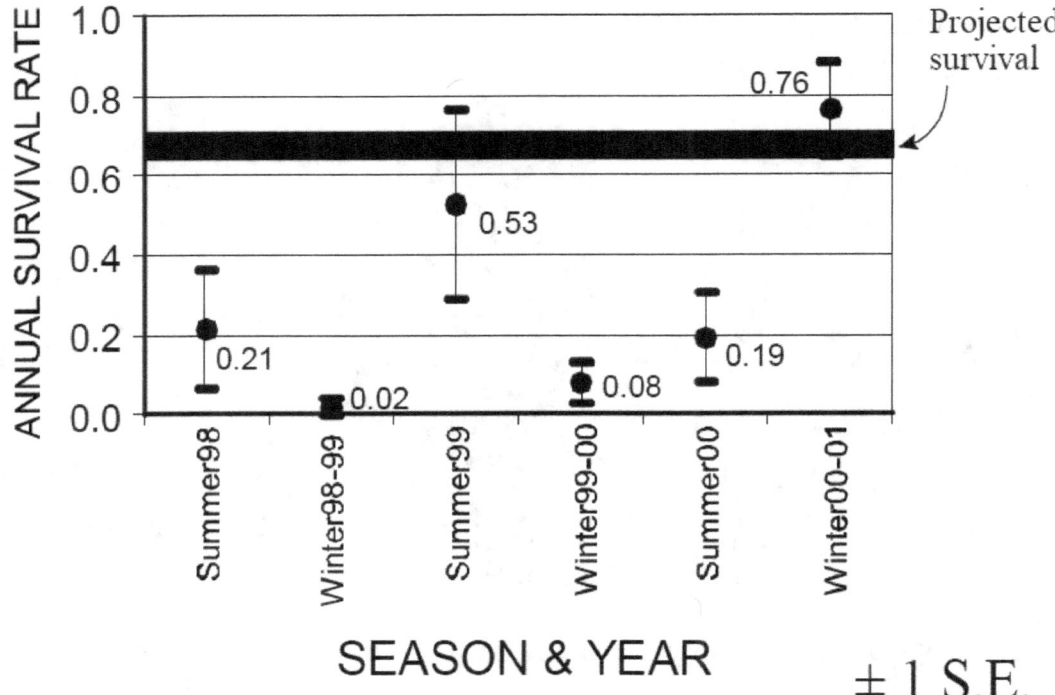

Figure 14. Survival analysis of reintroduced Mexican wolf population assuming that recapture represents a mortality event. Analysis was conducted for the period 1998-2001.

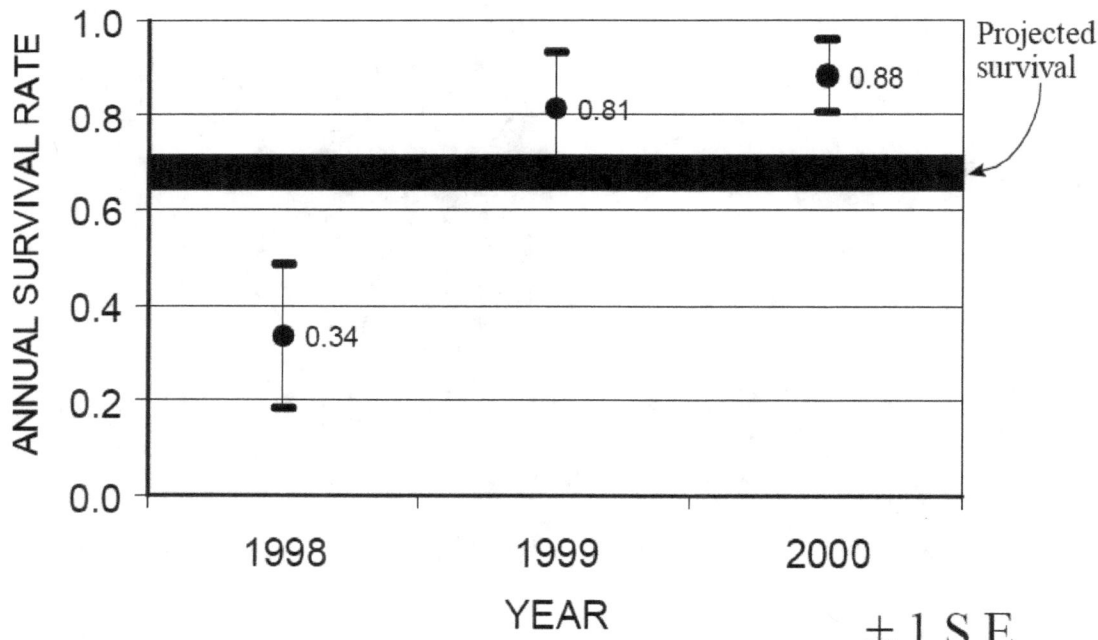

Figure 15. Survival analysis of reintroduced Mexican wolf population assuming that recaptures do not represent a mortality event. Analysis was conducted for the period 1998-2001.

e.   CONCLUSIONS

Frequent removals and re-releases of wolves confounded our analysis of rates and causes of mortality. However, if recaptured wolves were at high risk of being killed, then survival is much lower than projected in the EIS. Human-related deaths were the greatest source of mortality for reintroduced Mexican wolves. Shooting was the major source of death. Numerous other studies have reported human-caused deaths as the major cause of wolf mortality (Fuller and Keith 1980, Berg and Kuehn 1982, Boitani 1982, Carbyn 1982, Ballard *et al.* 1987, Fuller 1989, Mech 1989, Pletscher *et al.* 1997, and many others).

8.   IS POPULATION GROWTH SUBSTANTIALLY LOWER THAN PROJECTED IN THE EIS?

a.   BACKGROUND

Rates of increase in wild wolf populations have varied between 0.93 and 2.40 (Fuller and Keith 1980, Fritts and Mech 1981, Ballard *et al.* 1987, Hayes *et al.* 1991, Messier 1991, Pletscher *et al.* 1997). Several factors limit growth of wolf populations; those reported most commonly include ungulate biomass (Van Ballenberghe *et al.* 1975, Mech 1973, 1977a, 1977b, Fuller and Keith 1980, Packard and Mech 1980, Keith 1983, Messier 1985a, 1987, Peterson and Page 1988) and human-caused mortality (Van Ballenberghe 1981, Gasaway *et al.* 1983, Keith 1983, Peterson *et al.* 1984, Fuller 1989, Paquet *et al.* 1996, Noss *et al.* 1996). Keith calculated the maximum rate of increase for wolves ($r = 0.304$, $\sim = 1.36$) (1983) based on the highest reproductive and survival rates reported from studies on wild wolves. He corroborated the results by comparing the estimate with data from wolves that colonized Isle Royale National Park, 1952-1959 ($r = 0.304$, $\lambda = 1.39$). These were likely maximum rates of increase because the population was initiated by few individuals with abundant food (Keith 1983). However, both rates are still much lower than a theoretical exponential rate of 0.833 ($\lambda = 2.30$) given maximum reproduction (Rausch 1967), a stable age distribution and no deaths.

Keith (1983) suggested the amount of food available and age structure of the population affect rates of growth of wolf populations. VanBallenberghe (1981), Gasaway *et al.* (1983), Keith (1983), Peterson *et al.* (1984), Ballard *et al.* (1987), and Fuller (1989) found that wolf populations can be limited by harvest levels of 20-40%, but that the lower rate has a more significant effect in an area with low ungulate biomass (Gasaway *et al.*1983). Another factor to consider is that effects of harvest vary with time and population structure (Peterson *et al.* 1984, Fuller 1989). If productivity is high, and consequently the ratio of pups to adults is high, the population can withstand a higher overall mortality because pups (non-producers) make up a disproportionate amount of the harvest (Fuller 1989). Furthermore, net immigration or emigration may mitigate the effects of harvest (Fuller 1989).

b.   DATA SUMMARY

We assessed the density of the wolf population, size of established packs, and population growth using radiotelemetry data and direct observation by the Interagency Field Team. Most of these data are contained in the Monitoring and Events databases.

c.   METHODS

We calculated density of wolves/1000 km^2 by determining intra-pack densities (home range size/number of wolves in pack) of radio-collared wolves and averaging these densities per year (Potvin 1987, Bjorge and Gunson 1989, Okarma *et al.*1998). The size of packs was based on numbers of wolves observed during midwinter aerial locations (15 Jan-15 Feb). We estimated population growth using finite rates of increase (λ) based on the ratio of successive yearly estimates of density. Mean annual finite rate of increase was calculated by taking the antilogarithm of the mean exponential rate of increase ($\underline{r} = \ln \lambda$) for the population (Fuller 1989).

The fundamental equation of population demography for a closed population is:

$$N_t = N_{t-1} + B_t - D_t$$

where N_t = population size at time t, B_t = number of recruits at time t, D_t = number of deaths at time t,

For a wild population, removals are similar to mortality and re-releases similar to recruitment. Therefore, the equation that best describes the reintroduced Mexican wolf population is:

$$N_t = N_{t-1} + B_t - D_t + \beta_t - \delta_t$$

where δ_t = (unpredictable) removals of 'naughty' wolves, β_t = subsequent re-releases of those 'naughty' wolves, $\beta_t \gg B_t$, $\delta_t \gg D_t$

d.   RESULTS

From available databases and discussions with the Interagency Field Team, we identified a number of events relevant to assessment of population dynamics (Table 2). Using this information, we calculated population growth rates (Figures 16, 17) and the varying number of free-ranging wolves over time (Figures 18 and 19). Growth rates and numbers of wolves were close to projections, although frequent re-releases and removals obscured comparisons. To provide context for interpreting these results, we also generated mean growth rates for other reintroduced and recovering wolf populations (Figures 20, 21, 22). To date, the growth rate of the reintroduced Mexican wolf population is comparable with similar reintroduction and recovery efforts.

Table 2. Population events recorded for reintroduced Mexican wolf population between 1998 and 2001..

POPULATION EVENT	NUMBER
Recruits	3 - 5
Re-releases	21
Deaths	10 - 16
Removals	31

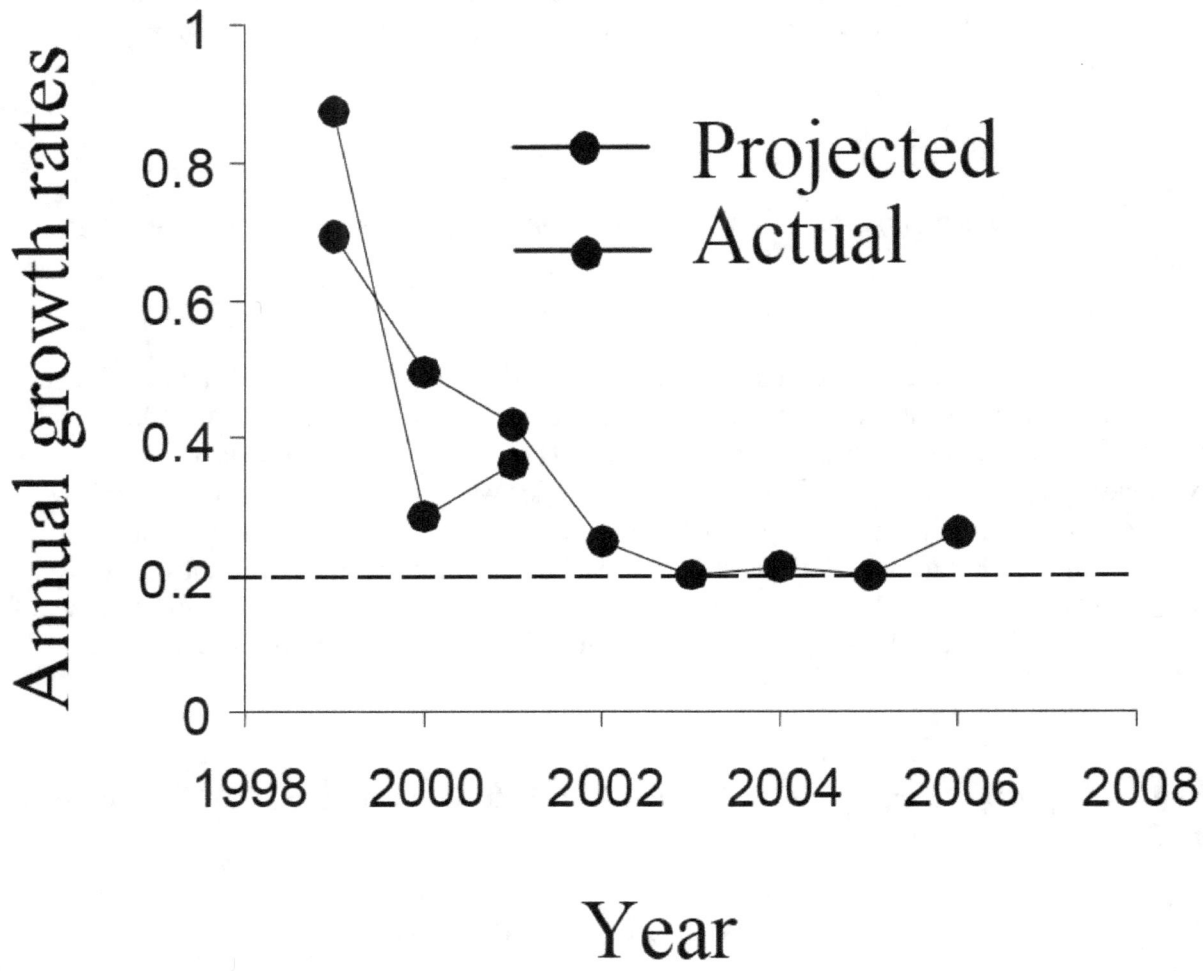

Figure 16. Projected and actual annual growth rates of free-ranging Mexican wolf population. Actual growth rate is strongly influenced by frequent intervention.

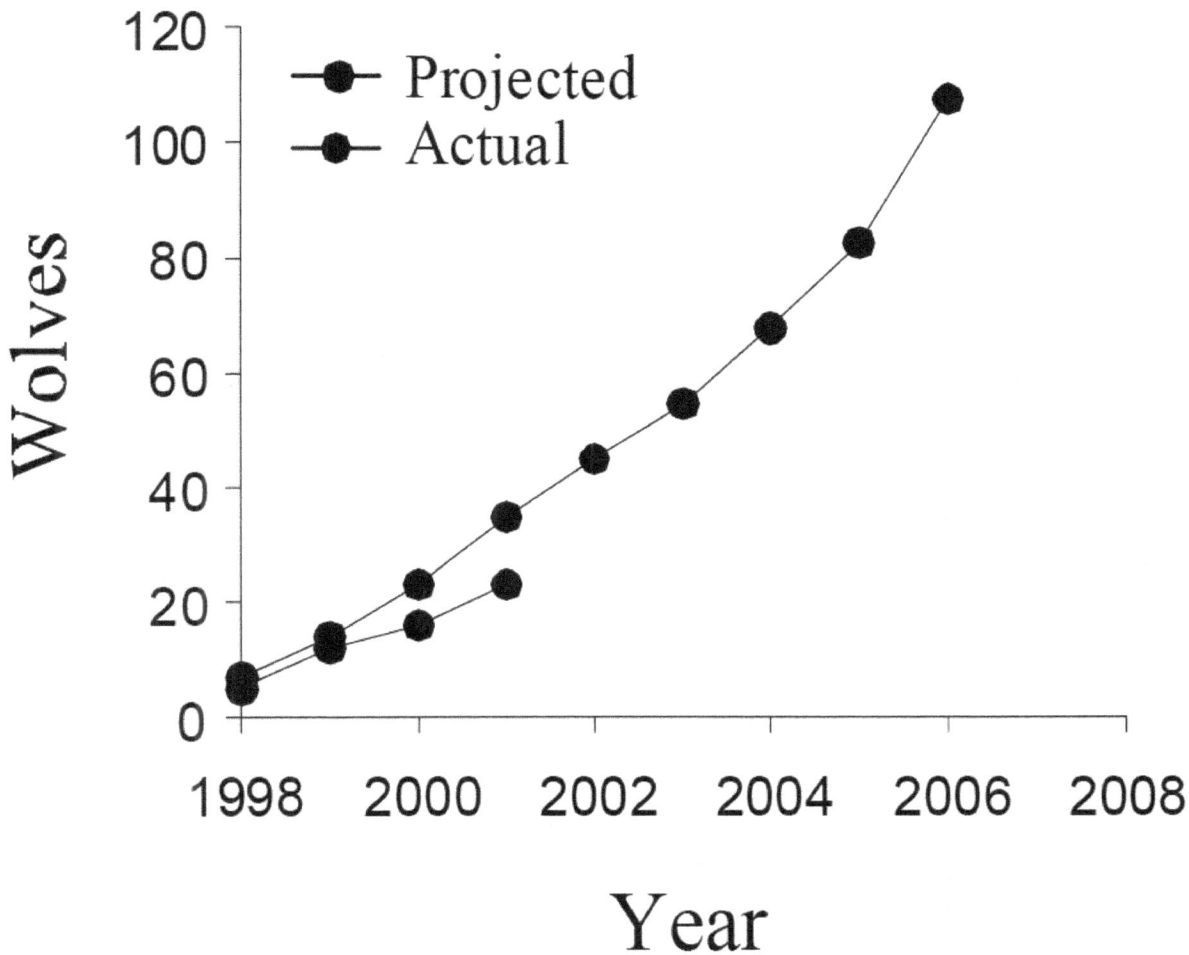

Figure 17. Projected and actual sizes of free-ranging Mexican wolf population, 1998-2001.

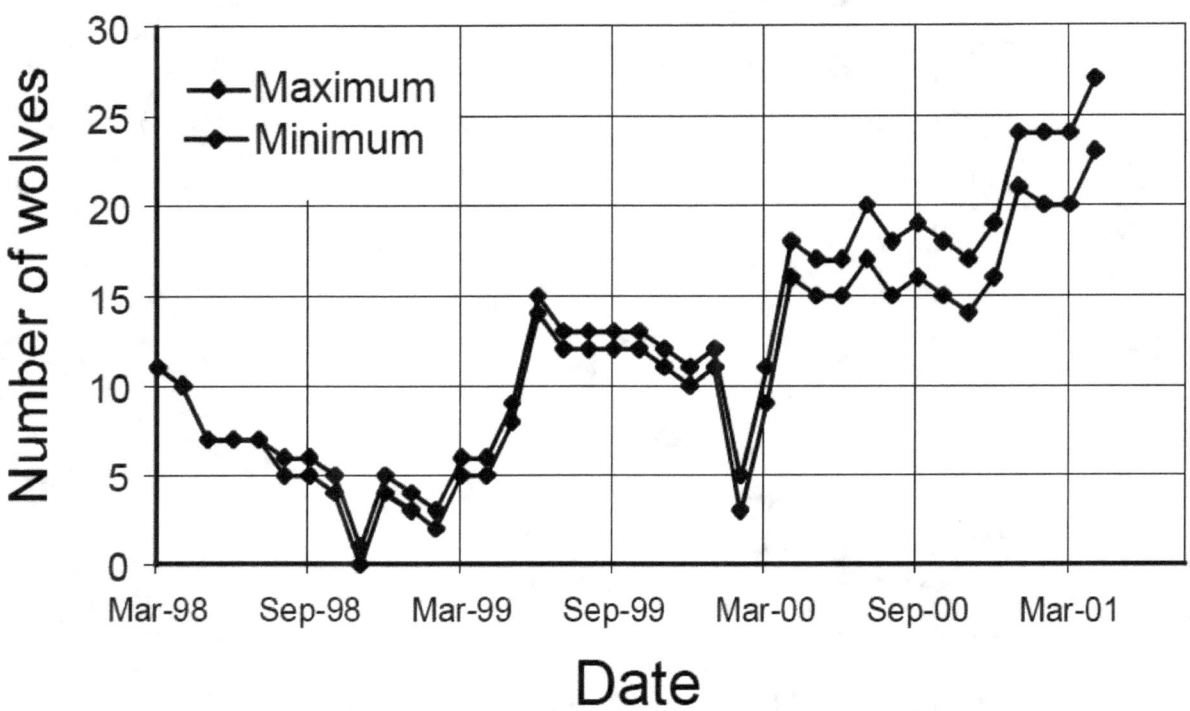

Figure 18. Number of free-ranging radiocollared Mexican wolves, 1998-2001. The difference between the max and min accounts for 4 wolves whose signals were lost, and in one case, a wolf that threw its collar.

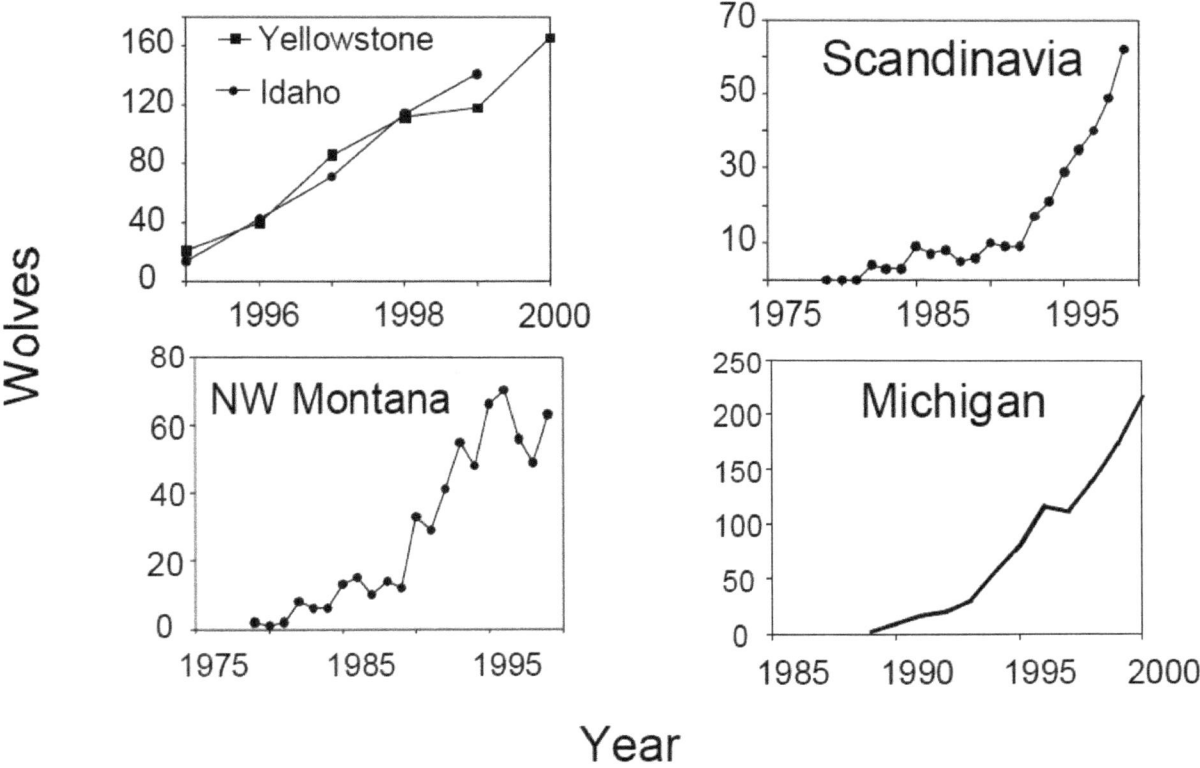

Figure 19. Growth rates of other recovering wolf populations. Sources: <http://www.r6.fws.gov/wolf/annualrpt99/> and unpublished documents from JAV

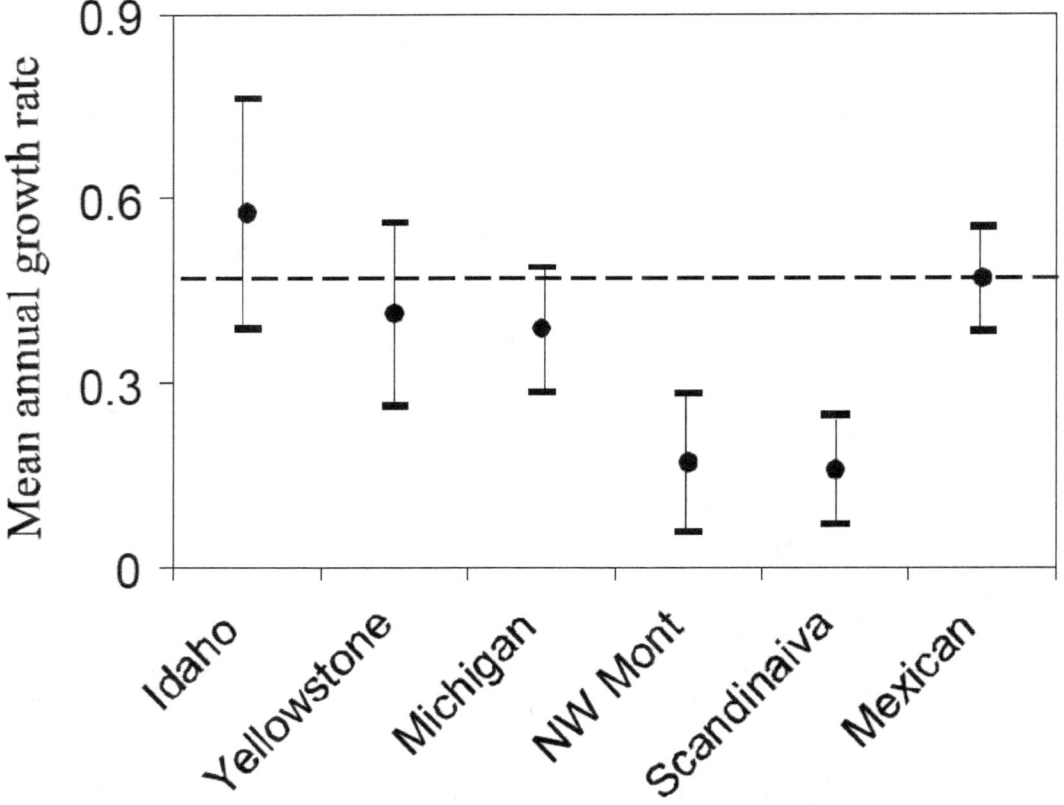

Figure 20. Mean annual growth rate for other recovering populations.

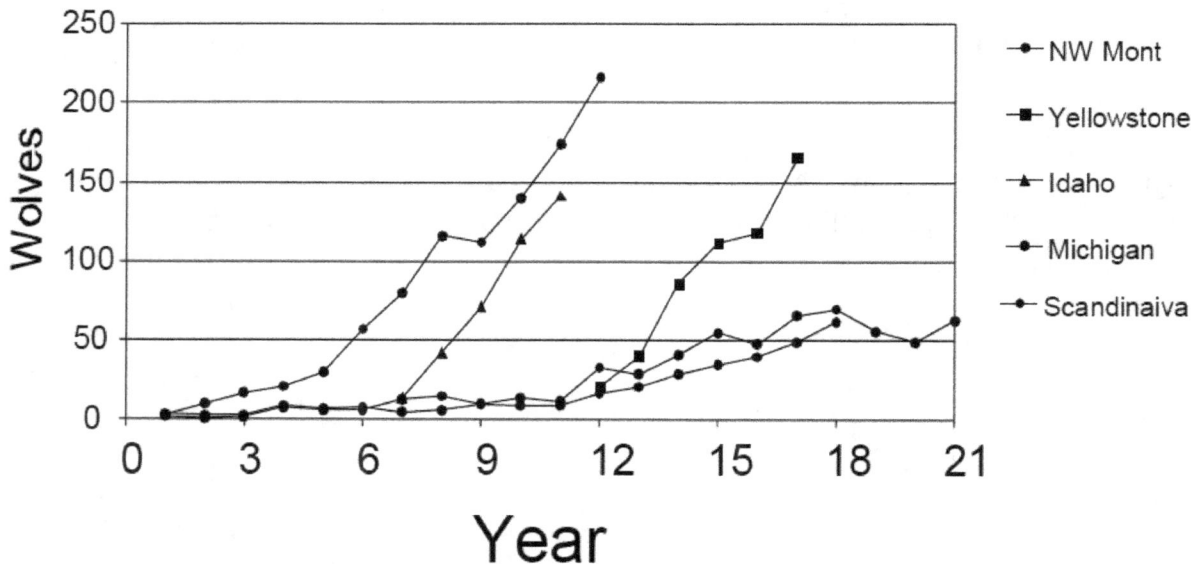

Figure 21. Number of wolves over time in other recovering populations.

Assessing the average growth rate only tells part of the story. Fluctuations in growth rates are also critical. The more fluctuation the greater the extinction risk. In this case, to assess fluctuations, we need to examine the population trajectory on a different time scale.

Using data collected since March 1998, we calculated a 39% chance that the annual growth rate is < 0.0; a 43% chance the annual growth rate is ≤ 0.10; and a 50% chance the annual growth rate ≤ 0.20 (Figure 22). Using data collected since December 1998, we calculated a 23% chance that the annual growth rate is < 0.0; a 26% chance the annual growth rate is ≤ 0.10; and a 29% chance annual growth rate ≤ 0.20 (Figure 23).

*A monthly growth rate of 0.083 corresponds to an annual growth rate of 0.1. A monthly growth rate of 0.0166 corresponds to an annual growth rate of ~0.2.

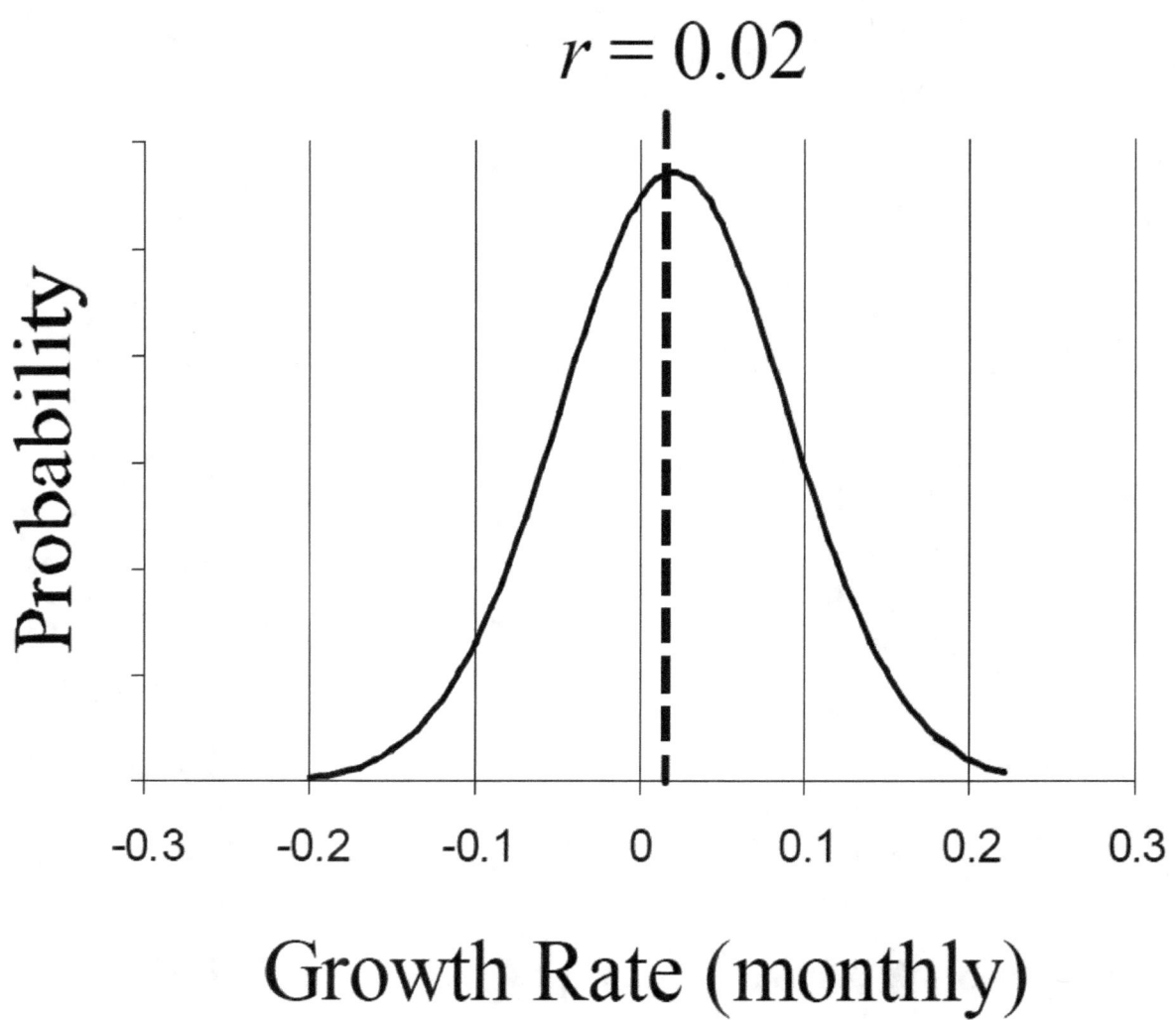

$r = 0.02$

Figure 22. Mean onthly growth rate (r) since March 1998. The expected value of r is 0.02. The standard error is 0.07.*

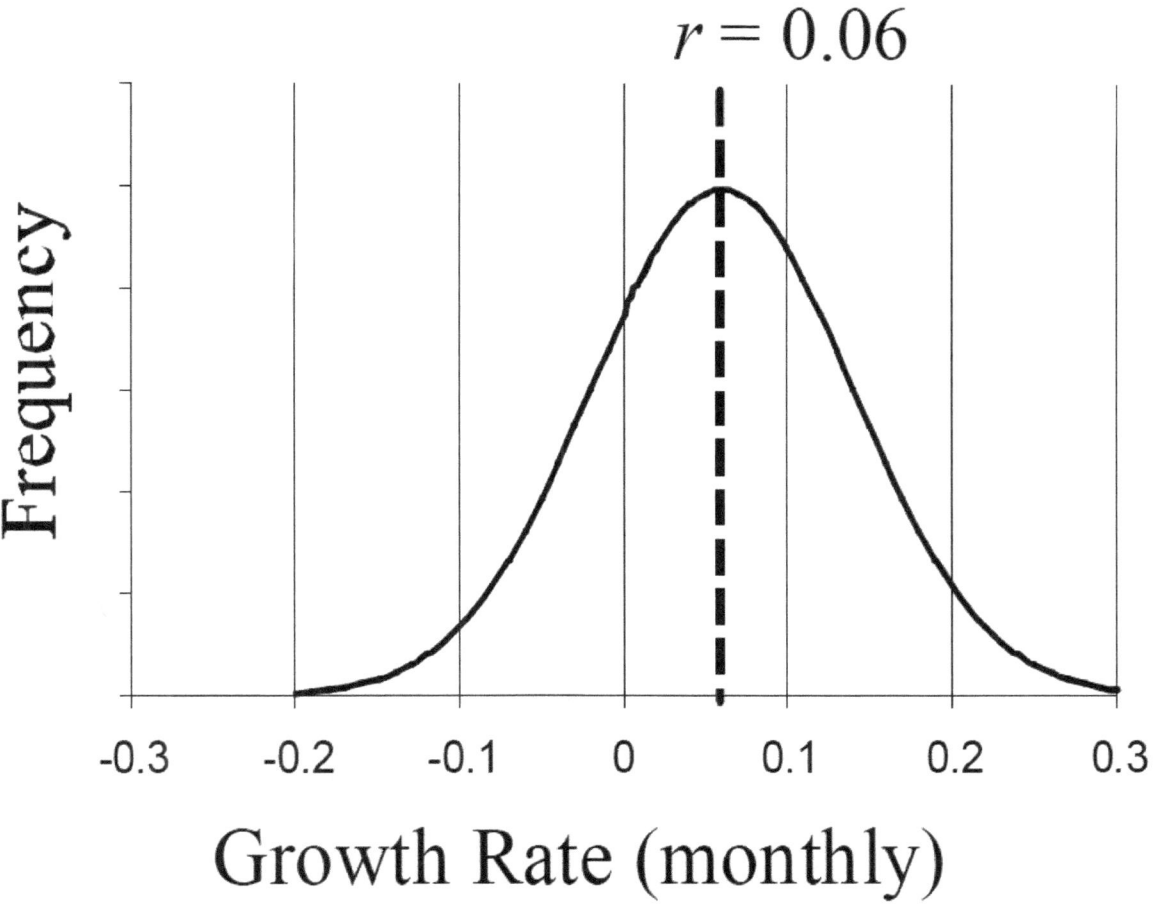

Figure 23. Mean monthly growth rate (r) since December 1998 (when population went temporarily extinct). The expected value of r is 0.06. The standard error is 0.08.

e.   CONCLUSIONS

To date, intervention has dominated natural processes. So, determining if the growth rate is lower than predicted in the EIS is not possible. If the current rate of intervention continues, restoration of a population of 100 wolves would require 28 re-releases annually and 41 removals annually. Although the current population size is similar to that projected in the EIS, we suspect that population growth would have fallen far short of expectations without intervention. Clearly, managers must balance future introductions, recaptures, and re-releases with the need to establish and maintain natural population processes (Figure 24).

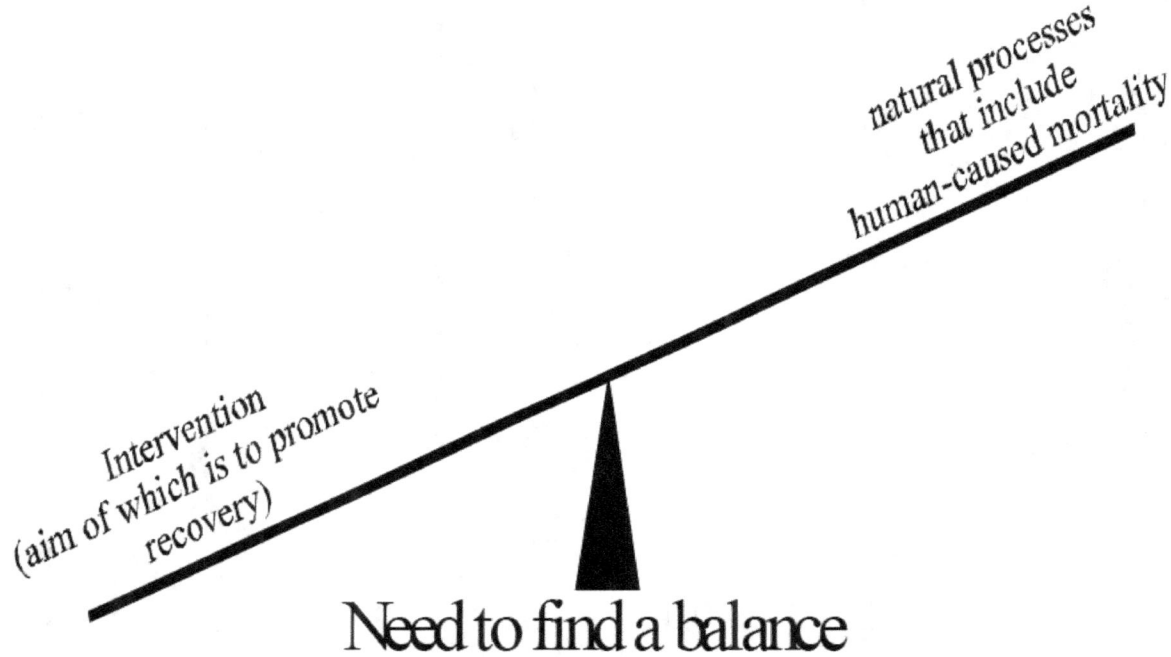

Figure 24. Because of frequent interventions the vital rates we derived (survival and population growth) are unlikley to reflect the population's future viability. A balance between intervention and the effects of natural population processes is needed.

9. ARE NUMBERS AND VULNERABILITY OF PREY ADEQUATE TO SUPPORT WOLVES?

a. BACKGROUND

Without human disturbance, densities reflect the wolf's dependency on ungulate prey species (Keith 1983). Wolf population dynamics are believed to be largely dictated by the per capita amount of prey and its vulnerability to predation, and the degree of human exploitation (Keith 1983; Fuller 1989). The effect of food on wolf demography is mediated by social factors, including pack formation, territorial behavior, exclusive breeding, deferred reproduction, intraspecific aggression, dispersal, and by primary prey shifts (Keith 1983).

Wolf populations are closely linked to population levels of their ungulate prey (Keith 1983, Messier 1985a, Fuller 1989). Maintaining viable, well-distributed wolf populations depends on maintaining an abundant, available, and stable ungulate population. Packard and Mech (1980) concluded that intrinsic social factors and the influence of food supply are interrelated in determining population levels of wolves. In situations where other factors reduce prey populations (e.g., winter weather), predation by wolves can inhibit the recovery of prey populations for long periods (Gasaway *et al.* 1983). In a multiprey system, the stability, or equilibrium, of ungulate prey and wolf populations seems to depend on a variety of factors, including the wolf predation rate, the number of ungulates killed by hunters, the ratio of ungulates to wolves, and the population growth rate of different ungulate species (Carbyn 1982, Huggard 1992, Paquet 1993, Paquet *et al.* 1996, Paquet 1989).

Changes in habitat composition and distribution can have a significant effect on prey densities and distributions, and therefore wolf spatial distribution. Wolf packs may react to changing conditions in varying ways, depending on the location of their territories in relation to other packs and prey distribution. If packs have lower prey densities within their territories, they may exploit territories more intensely.[3] This may be achieved by 1) persevering in each attack, 2) using carcasses thoroughly, 3) feeding on alternative and possibly second -choice food resources such as beaver (*Castor canadensis*) (Messier and Crete 1985), and 4) patrolling their territory more intensely (Messier 1985). Messier, in his study area in southeastern Quebec, found daily distances of Low Prey packs were on average either greater (summer) or equal (winter) to daily distances of High Prey packs. The territory size, however, was approximately 35% smaller in the Low Prey area, supporting the fact that wolves were searching each unit area with greater intensity in both seasons.

Many studies emphasize the direct effects (e.g., prey mortality) wolves have on the population dynamics of their ungulate prey (Carbyn 1974, Mech and Karns 1977, Carbyn 1983, Gasaway *et al.* 1983, Messier 1994, Messier and Crete 1985, Peterson *et al.* 1984, Gunson 1983,

---

[3] Territory and home range size is more closely correlated with pack size than with prey density (Messier 1985, Peterson *et al.* 1984). In areas of higher prey density pack sizes increase (Messier 1985). Messier's (1985) data indicate that between 0.2 and 0.4 moose/km^2, territory area per wolf is independent of moose abundance.

Ballard *et al.* 1987, Boutin 1992, and others). However, predation can also profoundly affect the behaviour of prey, including use of habitat, time of activity, foraging mode, diet, mating systems, and life histories (Sih *et al.* 1985). Accordingly, several studies describe the influence wolves have on movements, distribution, and habitat selection of caribou (*Rangifer tarandus*), moose, and white-tailed deer (Mech 1977, Stephens and Peterson 1987, Ballard *et al.* 1987, Nelson and Mech 1981, Messier and Barrette 1985, Messier 1994). Wolves can increase the rate at which they accrue resources by seeking out areas with dense concentrations of prey (Huggard 1991, Weaver 1994). Prey, in turn, can lower their expected mortality rate by preferentially residing in areas with few or no wolves. Several studies have suggested that ungulate prey seek out predator-free refugia to avoid predation by wolves (Mech 1977, Holt 1987, Paquet 1993). Wolf predation in the Superior National Forest of northern Minnesota was found to affect deer distributions within wolf territories (Mech 1977). Densities were greater along edges of territories where predation was thought to be less.

Unusually mild or severe winter weather can result in ungulate populations that are temporarily higher or lower than predicted habitat capability (which reflects long-term average maximum). Where predation is a factor, ungulates may exist at levels well below carrying capacity for relatively long periods. The interactions of ungulates and their predators (in our case wolves, coyotes, foxes, black bears, and cougars) may, under some circumstances, overshadow habitat capability as a controlling factor for ungulate populations. Ungulate populations may be more strongly influenced by the frequency and depth of population lows, than by habitat capability.

Ungulate biomass can affect rates of population increase and resulting densities of wolves. Building on work of Keith (1983), Fuller (1989) reviewed 25 studies of North American wolf and prey populations and found rates of increase of wolf populations are most affected by relative availability of ungulate biomass (directly influencing survival of pups <6 months old) and human-caused mortality. He concluded that regardless of prey type or stability of wolf populations, average wolf densities are clearly correlated with the biomass of ungulates available per wolf. Furthermore, he found the index of ungulate biomass per wolf is highest for heavily exploited (Ballard *et al.* 1987) or newly protected (Fritts and Mech 1981) wolf populations and lowest for unexploited wolf populations (Oosenbrug and Carbyn 1982, Mech 1986) or those where ungulates are heavily harvested (Kolenosky 1972).

b.   DATA SUMMARY
We used information in the carcasses database to assess wolf use of prey species. Prey densities and the weights of prey were derived from Groebner *et al.* (1995).

c.   METHODS
We estimated potential wolf numbers using regression equations that relate wolf numbers to ungulate biomass (Keith 1983, Fuller 1989). The equations were modified to reflect prey

species available to wolves in Arizona and New Mexico.[4] Accordingly, biomass was calculated by multiplying population densities of elk, white-tailed deer, and mule deer (*O. hemionus*) by average edible weights of elk, white-tailed deer, and mule deer. We used weights of 159 kg (350 lb.) for elk, 36 kg (80 lb.) for white-tailed deer, and 55 kg (122 lb.) for mule deer (Groebner *et al.* 1995). We used prey densities of 1.1 km² for elk, 0.9 km² for white-tailed deer, and 2.8 km² for mule deer (Groebner *et al.* 1995). Assuming that ungulate populations would decline slightly in the presence of wolf predation, prey densities were reduced 10% in our final calculations. We assumed prey were evenly distributed and equally available throughout the primary and secondary release sites. Bighorn Sheep (*Ovis canadensis*), pronghorn (*Antilocapra americana,* javelina (*Tayassu tayacu*), and beaver (*Castor canadensis*) were not included in our analyses because no population data were available.

 d. RESULTS

 The Interagency Field Team recorded 55 probable wolf kills. Elk constituted 85%, mule deer 7%, and deer of unknown species about 4% of recorded kills. The predominance of elk in the diet was consistent among packs (Figure 25). Based on numbers of prey available and biomass available within the primary release site, elk were used disproportionately. Note, however, that observational bias may skew collection of kill data. Elk are easier to find because they are larger than deer and not consumed as rapidly. In addition, the seasonal movements of wolves and their prey can affect spatial overlap and thus availability. Lack of data and time prevented us from assessing this possibility.

 Based on ungulate biomass, the Blue Range Wolf Recovery Area (6,854 mi² or 17,751 km²) can, in theory, support a an estimated 468 wolves (range 292-821). The target recovery area of 12,950 km² (5,000 km²) could support between-212 and 599 wolves (Figure 26) (Table 3). We believe these estimates are high because they assumes all prey are equal and will be consumed in proportion with availability. Given our experience with multiple prey systems elsewhere this is unlikely to occur. We therefore calculated wolf population estimates for individual prey species. Accordingly, elk in the Blue Range Wolf Recovery Area could support about 213 wolves, and the combined deer species about 255 wolves.

---

 [4]$Y = 0.041X$
where Y = wolf numbers, X = prey biomass

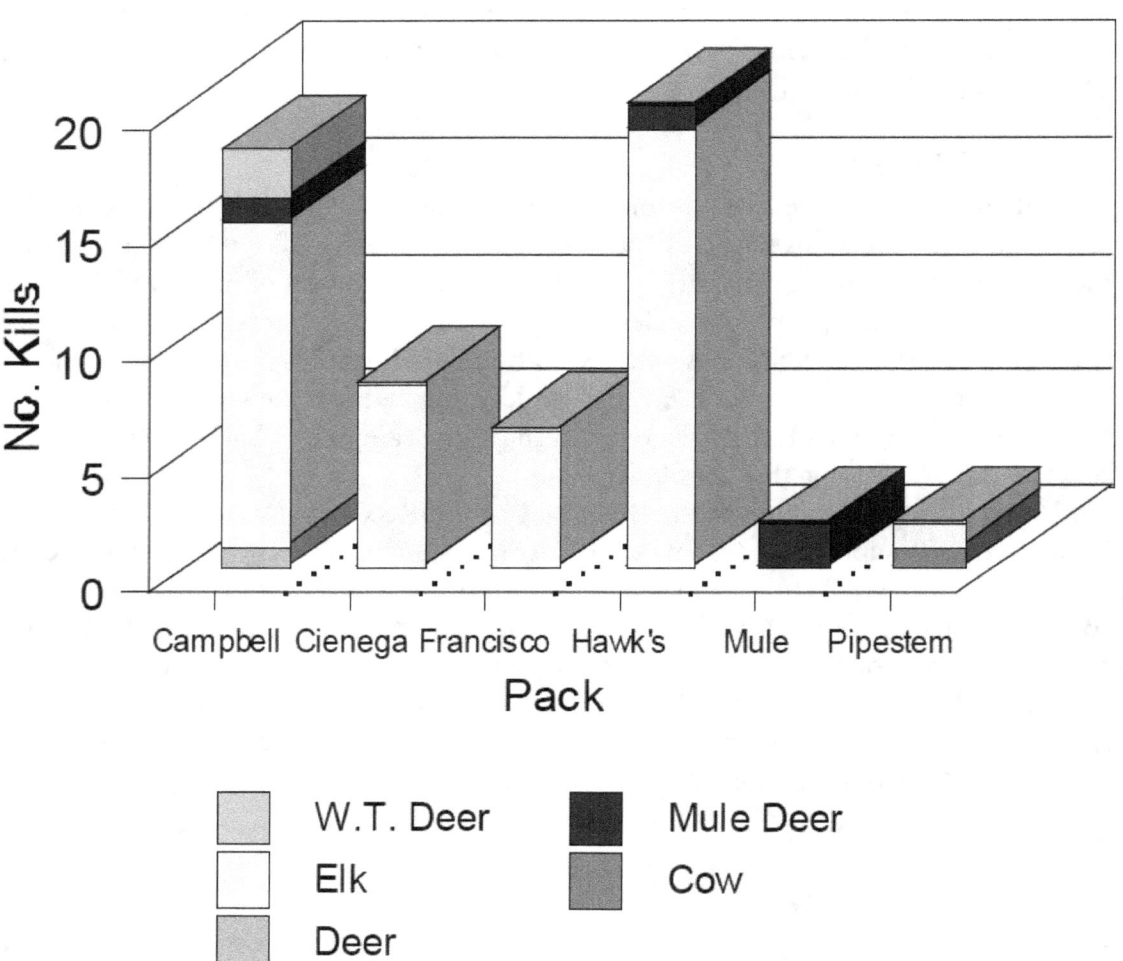

Figure 25. Prey (n = 55) probably killed by reintroduced Mexican wolves, 1998-2001.

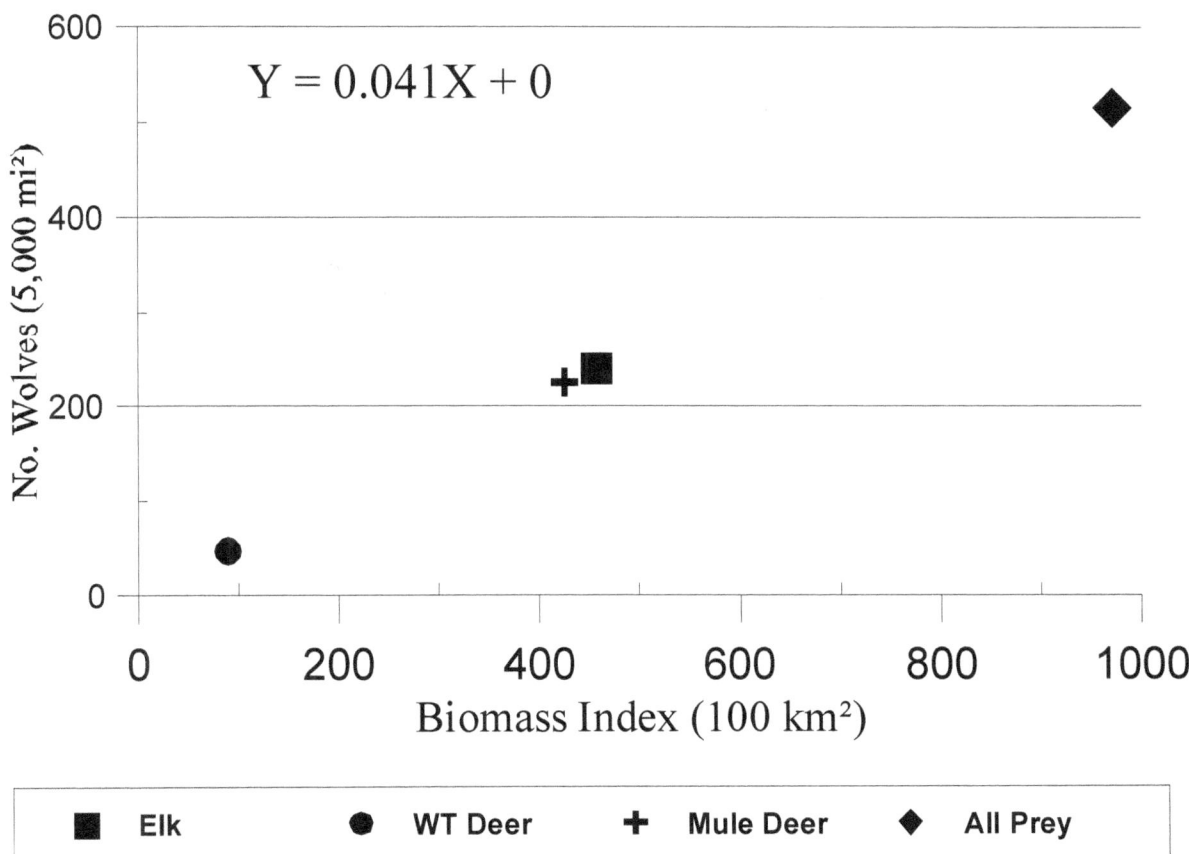

Figure 26. Potential number of wolves that, in theory, could occupy target objective of 12,950 km² (5,000 mi²) within the Blue Range Wolf Recovery Area. Estimates are based on prey biomass available to wolves and are maximum numbers. The individual contribution of ungulate prey species is shown for comparison with other studies.

Table 3. Potential wolf numbers (ranges) for recovery areas based on predicted population densities of ungulates 5 years post restoration of Mexican wolf population. We partitioned the table to show the contributions of different ungulate species.

PREY SPECIES	Primary Zone (2,664 km²)	Recovery Objective* (12,950 km²)	BRWRA* Low (17,563 km²)	BRWRA* High (17,563 km²)
White-tailed Deer	10-13			
Mule Deer	46-63			
White-tailed and Mule Deer		118-323	162-245	293-443
Elk	50-67	94-276	129-195	250-378
All Prey	106-143	212-599	292-441	543-821

*For white-tailed and mule deer, we used an average biomass.to derive wolf estimates.

e.   CONCLUSIONS

Given the current ratio of wolves to ungulate prey, we conclude the reintroduced Mexican wolf population is not limited by food. Adequate prey are available to support and sustain a growing wolf population. Estimated wolf numbers derived from ungulate biomass were similar to numbers projected in the EIS. Because wolves depend primarily on ungulates for food, long-term survival of wolves in the study region depends primarily on protection of habitat for elk and deer.

10. HAS THE LIVESTOCK DEPREDATION CONTROL PROGRAM BEEN EFFECTIVE?

a. BACKGROUND
Although an effective livestock depredation program is critical for wolf recovery, effective assessment of such a program requires more specific guidance and data than we were provided.

b. DATA SUMMARY AND METHODS
Our analysis is based on interpreting records in the Events and Incidences databases.

c. RESULTS
Forty-two (42) reports of possible wolf-livestock interactions were recorded between March 1998 and March 2001. Of these, the Interagency Field Team concluded that 5 events were accidents, 9 were non-wolf predators [e.g., bear (*Ursus americanus*), lion (*Felis concolor*), coyote (*C. latrans*)], 18 were wolf related, and 10 were probably wolf related. That is, 28 events involved wolves or probably involved wolves. These included uninjured livestock, injured livestock, and killed livestock (Table 4). The Interagency Field Team recorded 10 confirmed livestock-wolf interactions where no injury or death occurred. At a minimum, 55% (26) of all free-ranging wolves have interacted with livestock. Thirty-six percent (17) have interacted with livestock 3 or more times. Approximately 10% have interacted with livestock 5 or more times. Approximately three-quarters of the livestock injuries or deaths occurred on National Forests.

The number of reported livestock-wolf interactions varied seasonally (Figure 27). The interactions reported annually since the first reintroduction of Mexican wolves were; 5 from March 1998 to March 1999, 17 from March 1999 to March 2000, and 6 from Mar 2000 to Mar 2001.

Seventeen (17) reports of wolf interactions with cats or dogs were recorded between March 1998 and March 2001. These 17 reports included uninjured dogs, injured dogs, and killed dogs or cats. Of these, we concluded that; 13 interactions involved wolves; 1 interaction probably involved a wolf, and; 3 interactions cannot be classified using the data provided. The Interagency Field Team recorded 8 dog-wolf interactions where no injury or death occurred. Of the 13 interactions that definitely involved wolves, 5 resulted in the cat or dog being killed or injured (Table 5).

The average response time for all reported domestic animal-wolf interactions was less than 24 hours. The longest response time was 3 days, which occurred once.

Table 4. Numbers of domestic animal injuries and deaths due to wolf depredation. The data are for confirmed, probable and unconfirmed wolf depredations.

SPECIES	OUTCOME OF INTERACTION	
	Injured	Killed
Cow	1	5
Calf	2	8
Bull	1	1
Mini Colt	0	1
Lamb	0	1
Dog	3	1
Cat	0	1
Total	7	18

Table 5. Ownership of property where domestic animal injuries and death due to wolves took place. The data are for confirmed, probable, and unconfirmed wolf depredations.

OWNERSHIP	LIVESTOCK INJURIES OR DEATHS	CAT/DOG INJURIES OR DEATHS
National Forest	14	1
Private	3	2
Other or not recorded	2	2

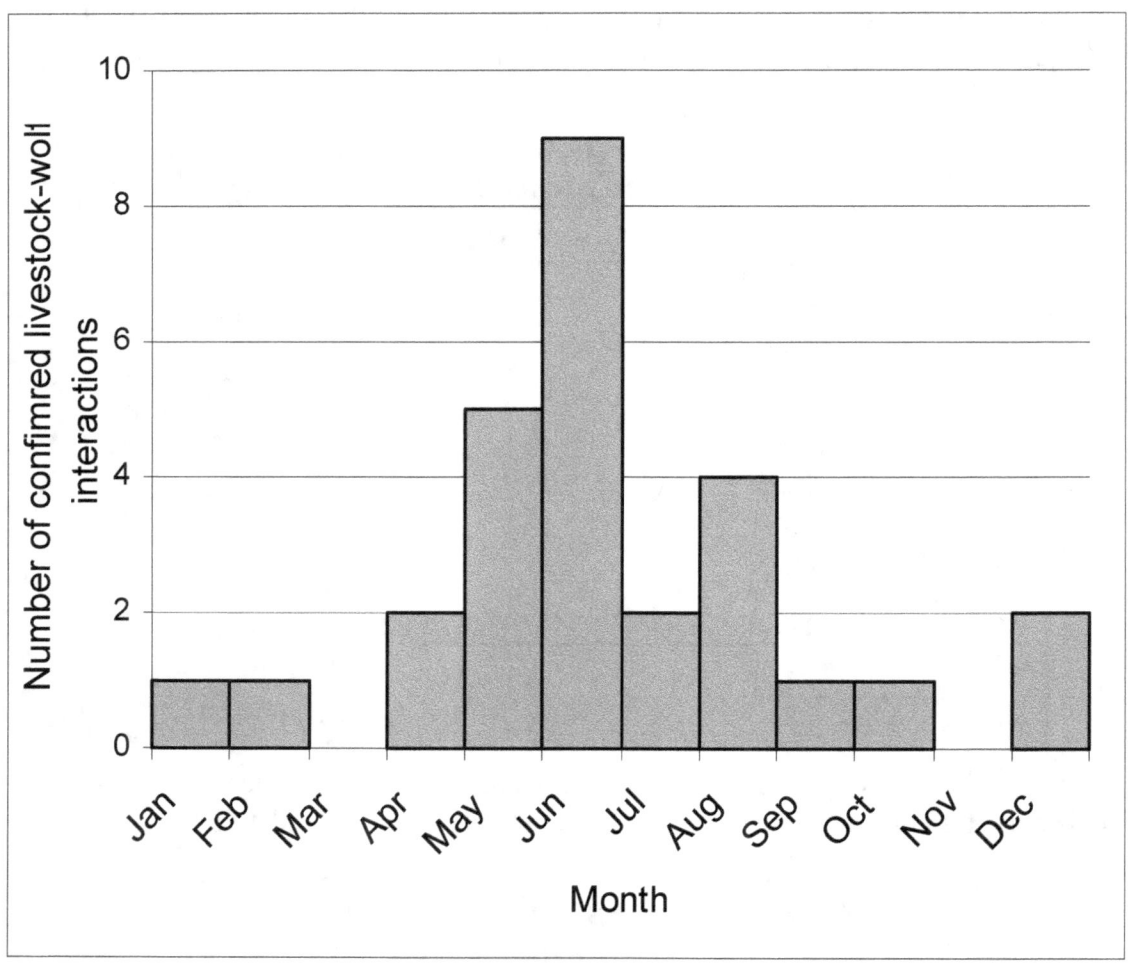

Figure 27. The number of livestock-wolf interactions fluctuated seasonally in the primary recovery zone.

d.   CONCLUSIONS

Livestock are omnipresent in the Blue Wolf reintroduction area. Because of the extensive temporal and spatial distribution of livestock, interactions with wolves are unavoidable. From the information made available to us, we believe the Service has been responsive to wolf-livestock and wolf-domestic animal conflicts. An equivalent level of responsive will be necessary in the future. Similarly, livestock producers using public lands can make a substantive contribution to reducing conflicts with wolves through improved husbandry and better management of carcasses.

11.   HAVE DOCUMENTED CASES OF THREATS TO HUMAN SAFETY OCCURRED?

Although no injuries or deaths have occurred, several wolf-human interactions have been reported. Consequently, evaluation of these incidences is largely qualitative based on our experiences with wolves in other parts of North America. We note that captive reared wolves released to the wild may behave differently than wild born wolves (Breitenemoser *et al.* in press).

a.   DATA SUMMARY AND METHODS

Our analysis of this issue is based on interpreting records in the Events and Incidences database.

b.   RESULTS

The Interagency Field Team reported eleven interactions between March 1998 and March 2001 (Table 6). On average, they reported one event every 3 months. However, the rate may be increasing (3 events from Mar 1998 to Mar 1999, 1 event from Mar 1999 to Mar 2000, 7 events from Mar 2000 to Mar 2001). If the rate is increasing, it is probably due to more wolves rather than an increased propensity for wolves to interact with humans. On average, one interaction was reported every 7 weeks from Mar 2000 to Mar 2001. Although data are too few to be certain, interactions do not seem to predominate in any particular time of the year.

Seven (of 11) interactions involved something that would be expected to attract wolves (e.g., dogs, deer carcass, livestock). Specifically, 5 (of these 7) involved dogs. One (of 11) interaction was instigated by the people involved (event #10). In 2 (of 11) events, the people involved *felt* as though their lives were threatened. In 4 (of the 11) events, an official response (i.e., from reintroduction personnel) occurred within 24 hours. In the other 7 events, no response date or time is reported. In 9 (of the 11) events, response involved an inspection of the site.

In 2 events (# 1 and #7), the people involved reported being fearful for their safety. However, experience suggests that because the people of event #7 responded appropriately, they were probably never in danger. In event #1, the wolf was shot. Event #8 is similar to cases in Ontario, British Columbia, and Alaska where wolves have injured people. In these all these cases, the people responded inappropriately to curious wolves or wolves attracted to food.

Twelve (12) different wolves have been involved with human interactions. Approximately 25% of all the wolves that have been released into the wild have been involved in a reported wolf-human ineraction. Eight (of these 12) wolves were involved in only a single event. One (of these 12) wolves (i.e., 590) was involved in 4 events. All these events took place in August and September of 2000. Since then, wolf 590 has not been involved in any human interactions. Three (of the 12) wolves (i.e., 587, 509, 511) were involved in 3 events. All 3 events included wolf 590.

The 'immediate' fate of the 12 wolves was: 1 shot, 2 brought into captivity, 1 brought into an acclimation pen, and in 8 cases no attempt was made to capture the wolf. The 'ultimate' fate of of the 12 wolves was: 2 shot, 3 permanently brought into captivity, 6 either are still free-ranging or died of natural causes, and for 1 wolf (i.e., #298, the potential data entry error) no data were available.

Table 6. Summary of wolf-human interactions reported for the Mexican wolf reintroduction program, 1998-2001.

EVENT	DATE	WOLVES INVOLVED	MEMO
1	April 28, 1998	156	Wolf 156 was shot by a camper who feared for his family's safety when the wolf came into their camp and attacked their dog.
2	May 8, 1998	494	494 became a nuisance frequenting the town of Alpine from 5/8/98 through 5/28/98 and was permanently removed from the wild.
3	January 6, 1999	166, 482	Campbell Blue pair jerked down a deer carcass hanging in some archery hunter's camp.
4	January 5, 2000	522	Female 522 hanging around hunters camp interacting with dogs. Trapped and put in acclimation pen to hold through hunting season.
5	April 14, 2000	166, 518	Dean Warren reported very aggressive encounter with Campbell Blue pair with the female, 518 bumping his horse and passing under it. Wolves also attacked one of his dogs. They followed him to cabin and he held up in it until the wolves left.
6	May 16, 2000	298, 191	Renee Dupree jogging with 2 dogs when 2 wolves approached -- wolves clearly interested in dogs. Renee scares wolves away.

7	August 20, 2000	511, 509, 587, 590	Don and his cocker spaniel were out in the middle of the meadow behind his trailer when 4 wolves (most likely Francisco) came tearing out of the woods towards them. Don fired 1 hot in front of the wolves but they kept coming ("one with a look of fierce determination"). He fired a second shot as they got closer and they reared away. He was very upset at the situation and felt that they were a danger to both people and animals/pets. Later that week, people camped nearby observed several wolves and pups resting in the shade under and around Don's trailer. At the time, he was inside watching golf with his dog, unaware that the wolves were outside. He was irrate when he learned of the incident, stating that this was not the behavior of wild animals and concerned about what would have happened had he or his dog come out of the trailer.
8	August 24, 2000	511, 509, 587, 590	Scott observed Francisco (and Cienega) on multiple occasions during his time camping at Double Cienega. Sometimes they came right through cmp < 5 ft of him taking pictures, although the pups seemed more skittish, other times farther away within the campground or out in the meadow. He also saw them once farther up Double Cienega and "the shaggy one" (yearling male 590) laid down w/in 10 ft and just looked at him while he took pictures.
9	September 25, 2000	590	Yearling male 590 hanging around Double Cienega Campground for the majority of the day.

| 10 | September 29, 2000 | 511, 509, 587, 590 | 5-6 people camped in Double Cienega from about 8/21-8/30/00. Throughout the week they interacted with Francisco. On multiple occasions they howled the pack in, chased them on ATVs, left food out, and shot blunt arrows at them. The wolves also chased their horses, mules, and the people in the ATVs. They were informed that this behavior was not acceptable, and we explained that what they were doing may possibly have negative effects on the wolves behavior. On 8/30/00, while speaking with the hunters, N. Sanchez observed the wolves chasing the mules. He then hazed the wolves by running at them and throwing rocks. They ignored him. We first spoke with the group on about 8/23/00. We informed them about the Mexican Wolf Recovery Project, the presence of wolves in the area, and proper behavior with respect to the wolves (ie. Do not leave out food; keep an eye on mules/ horses; if you see the wolves, yell and throw rocks at them.) We also told them to let us know if they had any interactions with the wolves. |
| 11 | October 1, 2000 | Unknown | At about 0440 Cole went out the front door on the porch and observed an animal in the driveway. At first he thought it was a German Shepard, then by the color and size he realized it was a wolf. He shewed it away and it headed west down the road. He tried to follow it in his truck but lost track of it. When he got back to the house it was by the back door eating out of the dog dish. He shewed it away again and it ran behind the house between the animal pens and the barn. He checked the dog dish and it was empty. He was not sure if there had been food in it or not. Stark and Grant responded to the call made by Ms. Leona Brown (the landowners sister). We looked at the area where the report was taken and observed large canid tracks in the driveway and yard. (track size=5x3 1/2", in sand and gravel). No other tracks were found in area. Stark and Armistead returned on 10/2 at about 0500. |

c. CONCLUSIONS

Wolf-human interactions have been reported consistently and regularly since the beginning of the program. Approximately 25% of the individuals in the free-ranging population have been involved with wolf-human interactions. As the wolf population grows, the Program should be prepared for steadily increasing frequencies of wolf-human interactions. Over time, the frequency of wolf-human interactions (per wolf) may decline with wild-born wolves that are less tolerant of humans. Because wolves can pass information between generations, the attraction to humans may take some time to extinguish. In the Republic of Georgia, for example, captive-born wolves were intensively trained to kill wild prey and to avoid humans before their reintroduction. This release procedure was considered successful after the third generation of wild-born wolves still showed the same behavior as their hand raised parents (J. Badrize pers. comm.).

The Program has responded well to wolf-human interactions, although documentation and data recording have been poor. For example, in the databases USFWS provided us no response dates or times were recorded for 7 events. It is critical that the Interagency Field Team keep comprehensive notes on wolf-human interactions. The Program should continue its practice of responding to all wolf-human interactions with immediate on site inspections and investigations. The Interagency Field Team appears to have made responsible decisions regarding the recapture of wolves involved in human interactions.

12. OVERALL CONCLUSIONS AND RECOMMENDATIONS

a. PREFACE

On 25 April we convened a meeting in Globe, Arizona to present our draft report to the Mexican Wolf Interagency Management Advisory Group (IMAG). We purposefully presented a draft to provide the IMAG a chance to make substantive contributions to our review. Many comments we received during the meeting clarified issues, thus materially improving our review. During the week of 30 April the draft report was, without our knowledge released to the media. During the following weeks several newspaper stories presented the findings of our draft review as final determinations. Moreover, on 12 May the Arizona Game and Fish Commission received a briefing about the reintroduction from representatives from the Arizona Game and Fish Department who also presented our draft findings as final determinations. Draft reports are by definition works in progress. Any discrepancy between the conclusions and recommendations presented in the draft report and those presented here are a result of that simple fact.

Our conclusions and recommendations are based on our analysis of the data. We believe the long term objective is to protect the wolf population and meet human needs by reducing the potential for one to seriously encroach upon the other. Current circumstances demand that wolves be conserved in a human dominated landscape. This requires a systematic and rigorous approach to wolf recovery that integrates the social and economic aspirations of humans with the ecological necessities of wolves.

b. CONCLUSIONS

The ultimate factor determining population viability for wolves is human attitude. Thus, an active and fully enabled Recovery Program comprising private interests, non governmental conservation organizations, local, state, federal, and tribal agencies is essential to ensure success of any restoration. The biology, politics, and sociology of wolf reintroduction in the Blue Range Wolf Recovery Area are too complex for recovery to be successful without a fully engaged and participatory Program. Fortunately, the Service has a successful history of reintroducing and effectively managing recovered wolf populations in other parts of the country (Refsnider 2000). Based on this success and the first 3 years of the Mexican wolf reintroduction, we think that expecting a similar outcome in the Blue Range Wolf Recovery Area is reasonable.

Overall we are satisfied with the progress of the reintroduction project since its inception in 1998. During May 2001, the Service reported that at least 28 wolves were free-ranging. Most of these animals are in social groups and the Service reports up to 5 litters have been produced in the wild this spring. Monitoring of reintroduced wolves has revealed that captive-born Mexican wolves can adjust to life in the wild by primarily preying on elk. This fact combined with the likely presence of several litters in the wild bodes well for the future. We believe the likelihood is high that continued application of the Service's current practices will result in the restoration of a self-sustaining population of Mexican wolves in the Blue Range Wolf Recovery Area. We believe, however, the Program should continue with some adjustments and modifications.

Not surprisingly, our review revealed room for improvement. Restoration of any wildlife population is fraught with uncertainty and work elsewhere shows that many projects are unsuccessful because of a failure to accommodate new information (Breitenmoser *et al.* in press). Several factors currently hinder recovery of a self-sustaining and viable wolf population. Those that predominate are:

1. The small areal extent of the primary recovery zone, which greatly hinders the vigor of the reintroduction phase of the reestablishment project
2. The Service's insistence that wolves only inhabit the small Blue Range Recovery area, which is at odds with the naturally extensive movements that characterize gray wolves and current thinking regarding the viability of large carnivore populations (Noss *et al.* 1996).
3. The Service's embrace of a target population of 100 wolves (EIS, page 2) when such a population is not viable over the long term (Shaffer 1987, IUCN 1994, Noss *et al.* 1996, Breitenmoser *et al.* in press).

    c.   RECOMMENDATIONS

The architects of the Mexican wolf reintroduction program properly accounted for the inevitable uncertainty and difficulty of the project by establishing adaptive management as the overarching operational paradigm. Consequently, our recommendations are largely the inevitable result of the reintroduction project's maturation. In this regard, we predict that the next review will also identify changes that can be made for improving the program..

If the Service adopts the recommendations presented below then the effectiveness of the reintroduction project and prospects for success will improve. Proper adoption of our recommendations will require a long-term and diligent effort by the Service. For many of the recommendations to be effective, biologists involved in the daily matters of the reintroduction effort must embrace them as standard operating procedures.

The current reintroduction project will greatly influence the future of the Mexican wolf recovery program since additional reintroduction projects will be required to remove *Canis lupus baileyi* from the list of endangered and threatened wildlife. Accordingly, we used our review to develop a few recommendations that consider Mexican wolf recovery overall. We also decided to consider programmatic issues that are germane to reintroduction, and issues the Service did not provide data for such as injuries resulting from capture. All of the recommendations below relate directly to the successful restoration of Mexican wolves the BRWRC. We did not elaborate on several biological issues, identified in our recommendations as important, because the reintroduction process is in too early a stage to have accumulated sufficient data.

Biological and Technical Aspects

WE RECOMMEND THAT THE SERVICE:

Continue to develop appropriate opportunities to release (and re-release) wolves for at least 2 years to ensure the restoration of a self-sustaining population.

Begin developing population estimation techniques that are not based exclusively on telemetric monitoring. As the wolf population grows it will become increasingly difficult to maintain telemetric contact with all known or suspected packs. Consequently, the Service needs to develop non-telemetrically-based methodology (e.g., track station surveys, genetic sampling of hair or fecal material) for assessing the distribution and size of the wolf population.

Develop data collection forms and data collection and management procedures similar to those used by the red wolf restoration program in North Carolina.

Require biologist to promptly and carefully enter field data into a computer program for storage and analysis. The Service should require biologists to record data on a per wolf and per day basis. Data checking should be improved to eliminate data entry errors. In this regard, picklists and auto filling fields can simplify data entry and improve accuracy. Lastly, the Service should require that data files be proofed at least once before they conduct analyses. We remind field biologist working on the project that generally 1 hour of productive time in the field requires 2 hours in the office for data management and initial analyses.

Make all data available for research and peer review.

Carefully consider using a modified #3 soft-catch trap for capturing Mexican wolves rather than the McBride #7. We are concerned that the #7 might cause unacceptably frequent and serious foot injuries. The Service might find that a modified #3 soft-catch trap is more appropriate for capturing wolves that have a high probability of being re-released or that are fairly small (e.g., smallish adults or pups). Modified soft-catch traps have been used to capture hundreds of red wolves that are similar in size to Mexican wolves and larger gray wolves (Quebec) with no serious foot injuries (M. Phillips unpublished data, P. Paquet unpublished data). However, careful consideration of all aspects of capturing wolves with leghold traps will lead to a proper decision about the use of a modified trap for capturing Mexican wolves.

Encourage research that will help to inform future Program evaluations and adjustments. The research we suggest is beyond the scope of the current Mexican wolf program because of resource limitations (personnel and fiscal) and the need to focus on the central mission of reintroducing wolves. However, research partnerships with universities and other organizations should be developed. Increasing the capacity of the Mexican wolf recovery Program, should be a principle charge of the Recovery Team. The following areas are of contemporary conservation and academic interest and should be research priorities:
1. Population modeling (PVA and metapopulation model) and sensitivity analysis of short- and long-term demography and distribution
1. Assessment of new threats to population including new guild structure, disease, and human activity.
2. Habitat viability analyses of the release area and projected population range (environment, resources, carrying capacity, spatial characteristics, etc.)
3. Development of guidelines for decision-making in conflict situations
4. Reassessment of policies for intervention in the release phase
5. Assessment of monitoring programs

6.   Evaluation and design of long-term management program, including
       a.   Evaluation design of long-term monitoring program
            1.   demography and population range
            2.   genetic surveillance
            3.   health surveillance
            4.   long-term adaptation of individuals and population to ecosystem
            5.   effects on ecosystem (predation, displacement)

7.   The interaction of Mexican wolves with other carnivores in the reintroduction area. Reintroduction or recolonization of wolves influences the behavior, abundance, and distribution of other carnivore species. For example, wolf recovery in the Rocky Mountains has resulted in interference and exploitation competition among wolves, bears, coyotes, and cougars, causing changes in the composition and structure of the carnivore guild.

Develop a contemporary definition of a biologically successful wolf reintroduction and the criteria needed to measure success. The latter includes methods and time scales. Specific issues that need to be considered are:

1.   How many wolves and how many breeding pairs will result in a demographically and genetically viable population?
2.   How do metapopulation dynamics affect the viability of Mexican wolves?
3.   How broad a geographic area would such a population inhabit?
4.   What affect will a viable population have on elk, deer, cattle, etc.?
5.   What target population size will lead to long-term demographic viability?
6.   What target population size will lead to long-term genetic viability?

We propose the application of the IUCN Red List Categories (IUCN 1994) to assess success and failure at 5 and 10 years following completion of the release phase (Table 7). The classification is based on an assessment using 5 criteria; population reduction, area of occurrence and occupancy, 2 criteria for population density, and a quantitative analysis of the extinction probability. If the population is assessed as "critically endangered" after 10 years the project should be considered a failure because there is a very high risk of extinction in the wild in the future. The minimum standard for success should be vulnerable or better. Vulnerable populations still face a high risk of extinction in the medium-term future and require ongoing management.

Table 7. Biological criteria for measuring project success of Mexican wolf reintroduction at about 5 and 10 years following completion of reintroduction phase. If the evaluation falls between failure and success, the viability of the population should be classified as uncertain. These guidelines follow the Red List Categories (IUCN 1994: www.iucn.org/themes/ssc/redlists/ssc-rl-c.htm)

CRITERIA	FAILURE	SUCCESS

Population reduction of x%, projected or suspected within the next 10 years.	> 80%	< 20%
Extent of occurrence estimated to be x km² or area of occupancy estimated to be y km², and estimates indicating 2 of the following: (1) severely fragmented or known to exist in only one location; (2) projected decline or extreme fluctuations in extent of occurrence, area of occupancy, habitat area or quality, number of locations or subpopulations, or number of mature individuals; (3) continuous, observed, inferred or projected decline in area, extent or quality of habitat.	$x < 100$ $y < 10$	$x \geq 5,000$ $y \geq 500$
Population estimated to number x mature individuals and projected continuous decline in number of mature individuals, and population severely fragmented or all individuals in a single population	$x < 250$	$x \geq 250$
Population estimated to number x mature individuals.	$x = 50$	$x \geq 250$
Probability of extinction is x within ye years or z generations, whichever is longer.	$x \geq 50\%$ $y = 10, z = 3$	$x < 20\%$ $y = 20, z = 5$

Valuational and Organizational Aspects

WE RECOMMEND THAT THE SERVICE:

Modify the recovery team by inviting an appropriate individual other than the recovery coordinator to serve as the team leader. While ultimate responsibility for Mexican wolf recovery would still reside with the recovery coordinator, enlisting another individual to serve as team leader would increase the capacity of the recovery program. Other recover program use this administrative structure and it works well (e.g., the California condor recovery program).

Instruct the modified recovery team to revise by June 2002 the 1982 recovery plan. A revision of the recovery plan is long overdue for several reasons. First, the current plan does not contain any standards for removing *C. l. baileyi* from the endangered species list. Second, since the plan was approved great advances have been made in the science of conservation biology; such advances would greatly instruct revision of the recovery plan. Finally, due to work with red wolves in the southeast, gray wolves in the Great Lakes states and the northern Rockies, and Mexican wolves in the Blue Range Wolf Recovery Area we have a much greater understanding of wolf reintroductions and management; such understanding would greatly inform revision of the Mexican wolf recovery plan.

Immediately engage the services of the modified recovery team. The challenges of wolf restoration are many and varied. Meeting such challenges requires a restoration effort that is itself diverse and capable. The current reintroduction project and Mexican wolf recovery in general would benefit substantially from the efforts of a fully engaged recovery team.

Immediately modify the final rule (Parsons 1998) and develop the authority to conduct initial releases into the Gila National Forest. Several releases conducted during the first 3 years of the reintroduction project resulted in wolves settling much of the primary recovery zone in the Blue Range Wolf Recovery Area. As work elsewhere (Phillips unpublished data) has revealed, wolves should not be released in areas that support resident animals. Over time, it will become harder for the Service to find suitable release sites in the primary recovery zone. The Service can best address this problem by obtaining the authority to conduct initial release in the secondary recovery zone, most notably the Gila National Forest. This recommendation was first made to the Service by a panel of experts (including Phillips) enlisted by the Service to review the reintroduction program in January 1999. Despite the Service's approval of the recommendation, they have taken no implementation action. This is by far the most important and simplest change the Service can make to the existing reintroduction project. The Gila National Forest is approximately 75% of the 4.4 million acre Blue Range Wolf Recovery Area. The Gila Forest includes about 700,000 acres that are roadless and free of livestock. Several high-quality release sites are available in the area. Using them is the best way for improving the cost-effectiveness and certainty of the reintroduction project. Accordingly, we strongly recommend that the Service immediately take whatever action is necessary to conduct initial releases of captive-born (and wild-born if appropriate) Mexican wolves to the Gila National Forest.

Immediately modify the final rule to allow wolves that are not management problems to establish territories outside the Blue Range Wolf Recovery Area. For specific language and instruction for this modification we strongly recommend that the Mexican wolf recovery program review the final rule promulgated for the gray wolf recovery in the northern Rockies (Bangs 1994). During the first 3 years of the reintroduction the Service recaptured some Mexican wolves simply because they left the Blue Range Wolf Recovery Area. As the wolf population grows, more animals will disperse from the Blue Range Wolf Recovery Area. Retrieving animals because they wander outside the primary recovery area is is inappropriate because it is:

1.   inconsistent with the Service's approach to recover wolves in the southeast, Great Lakes states, and the northern Rockies;
2.   will lead to serious logistical and credibility problems as the wolf population grows and more wolves disperse from the area; and
3.   needlessly excludes habitat that could substantially contribute to recovery of *Canis lupus baileyi*.

Before the current Mexican wolf reintroduction project was initiated, the red wolf recovery program adopted a similar approach (Henry 1995) with dire consequences (Phillips and Smith 1998). Extensive tracts of public land and some private land outside the Blue Range Wolf Recovery Area are suitable for wolves. Consequently, we strongly recommend that the Service develop the appropriate flexibility to allow wolves to occupy lands outside the Blue Range Wolf Recovery Area. We believe that obtaining the requisite flexibility will require that the Service modify the final rule currently governing the reintroduction project.

We recognize that the statements above as they relate to private land may cause controversy so we offer the following remarks. Allowing Mexican wolves to inhabit suitable tracts of private land (e.g., large holdings) in the absence of problems, would bring the reintroduction project into compliance with Service-led efforts to recover wolves elsewhere. Allowing wolves to inhabit private property in the absence of a problem should not be construed to mean that the Service would begin to actively target private lands as wolf habitat that needs to be settled. Quite the contrary, and note that nowhere is the Service effecting management of private land to promote wolf conservation. However, throughout the U.S (except in the Blue Range Wolf Recovery Area) if a wolf wanders onto private property and does not cause a definable problem, and its mere presence is not a definable problem, then the Service is not required to remove the animal even if the landowner demands such action.

Such an approach to wolf recovery is consistent with the determination in the United States that the public owns wildlife, rather than private landowners. Within limits, landowners can manage their property in a way that promotes or hinders the welfare of wildlife. However, through laws enforced by state and federal officials, citizens decide under what circumstances wildlife can be captured and moved or killed from public and private land. Such decisions are not the prerogatives of the landowner, regardless of whether the animal(s) in question are naturally occurring or present because of a reintroduction program.

In sharp contrast with the Service's approach elsewhere, the Mexican wolf project developed a rule that requires wolves to be removed from public and private land outside the Blue Range Wolf Recovery Area, even in the absence of a problem (Parsons 1998). Such regulations are inappropriate for at least 2 reasons: 1) they are nearly impossible to effectively carry out as the wolf population grows because of the difficulties of managing an ever-increasing number of wide-ranging dispersing animals, and 2) they establish a precedent that could be effectively used to argue for the removal of other endangered species inhabiting certain tracts of public or private land.

Certainly local opposition to the Mexican wolf reintroduction program affected the development of such a rule. Indeed, the recovery program coordinator assumed from personal knowledge of local politics and sentiments that a more restrictive rule would have significantly hindered and possibly caused the termination of the project (D. R. Parsons personal communication 1996). Maybe this was a valid assumption. Opinion polls, however, suggest widespread and persistent local support for wolf recovery in the southwest (Duda and Young 1995, Pate *et al.* 1996, Meadows 2001). Regardless, noting that wolf recovery elsewhere has faced substantial opposition is instructive, but the Service did not promulgate similarly onerous rules (e.g., see Bangs 1994, Henry 1995). And to date, recovery efforts elsewhere have been quite successful (Refsnider 2000).

Resist any opportunity to reintroduce Mexican wolves in the White Sands Wolf Recovery Area (WSWRA). Two independent assessments suggest that the WSWRA could support only 20 to 30 wolves (Bednarz 1989, Green-Hammond 1994); such a population is not viable (Shaffer 1987). The inability of the WSWRA to support a viable population of wolves is due to the area's relative smallness (about 10,311 km² or 4,028 mi²) and its distance from other suitable habitat. For example, the WSWRA is about 100 km (62 miles) from the extreme eastern edge of the BRWRA. While wolves can easily traverse such a distance, the "dispersal area" comprises very poor wolf habitat, supports the town of Truth or Consequences, New Mexico in its core, and is bisected by the heavily traveled federal Interstate 25. Accordingly, the USFWS should not expend resources on reintroducing wolves to the WSRWA.

Provide biologists with opportunities to visit other wolf projects to gain training with capturing and handling free-ranging and captive wolves.

Station the field coordinator in the Blue Range Wolf Recovery Area (e.g., in Glenwood or Silver City, New Mexico or Alpine, Arizona) and insist that this person be intimately involved with all aspects of fieldwork (wolf management; public relations; data collection, management, analysis, report preparation; etc.). We think it would be a serious mistake to station the field coordinator in the Regional Office in Albuquerque. Such a decision would add a level of complexity that is entirely unwarranted.

Put forth a concerted effort to develop realistic expectations for the project. Restoration is an imprecise process that is by definition "heavy-handed". The Service needs to constantly remind the public and the media of this fact. It is certain that the Service will have to overcome great challenges in the future. Such challenges will mean that intervention will be required, that wolves will disappear, and that some animals will die. But just as certainly, meeting the challenges will ensure the restoration of a self-sustaining population of Mexican wolves in the Blue Range Wolf Recovery Area.

Initiate programs to educate people about wolf behavior. In most events involving humans, wolves are interested in dogs or food (e.g., carcasses, dog food, etc.). Members of the program expected to respond to wolf-human interactions should be well educated on the nature and variety of reports from Algonquin provincial park, Alaska, and British Columbia. The Program should contact other western communities and agencies that have dealt with large carnivore-human interactions (e.g., mountain lions, bears, wolves). The Program should also actively warn people that dogs, deer/elk carcasses, and livestock carcasses may attract wolves. Although the danger is not the same, hunters should be advised to behave as though they are in grizzly bear country.

Require livestock operators on public land to take some responsibility for carcass management/disposal to reduce the likelihood that wolves become habituated to feeding on livestock. Currently livestock grazing is permitted on about 66% of the Blue Range Wolf Recovery Area. At least 3 packs were removed from the wild because they scavenged on dead livestock left on national forest lands. Such scavenging may predispose wolves to eventually prey on livestock. Accordingly, reducing the wolves' access to carcasses will greatly facilitate coexistence between ranchers and wolves in this portion of the recovery area carcasses.

While some predation on livestock is inevitable, reasonable means of reducing the frequency of occurrence will enhance wolf recovery so that is respectful of the needs and concerns of livestock producers. Consequently, livestock producers using public land in occupied Mexican wolf range should be required to exercise reasonable diligence in finding livestock that have died to either dispose of the carcass or enable the Service to do so. Such diligence will probably reduce predation on livestock, which in turn will improve the cost-effectiveness and certainty of the reintroduction project.

When writing or lecturing about the project, the Service should emphasize a community approach to understanding the wolf reintroduction project and its effect on other species and ecological processes. Conservation policy is shifting away from the preservation of single species toward preservation and management of interactive networks and large-scale ecosystems on which species depend. It is extremely important that the Service view the wolf reintroduction program in this context.

BIBLIOGRPAHY AND LITERATURE CITED

Alexandre, A., J. P. Barde, C. Lamure and F. J. Langdon.. 1975. Road Traffic Noise. Halsted Press, Wiley & Sons. New York.

Ballard, W. B. and J. R. Dau. 1983. Characteristics of gray wolf, *Canis lupus*, den and rendezvous sites in southcentral Alaska. Canadian Field Naturalist 97:299–302.

Ballard, W. B., J. S. Whitman, and C. L. Gardner. 1987. Ecology of an exploited wolf population in south-central Alaska. Wildlife Monographs 98.

Ballard, W. B., L. A. Ayres, P. R. Krausman, D. J. Reed, and S. G. Fancy. 1997. Ecology of wolves in relation to a migratory caribou herd in northwest Alaska. Wildlife Monographs 135.

Bangs, E. E. 1994. Establishment of a nonessential experimental population of gray wolves in Yellowstone National Park in Wyoming, Idaho, and Montana – final rule. Federal Register 59:60252-60281.

Bangs, E. E., and S. H. Fritts. 1996. Reintroducing the gray wolf into central Idaho and Yellowstone National Park. Wildlife Society Bulletin 24:402-413.

Bednarz, J. C. 1998. An evaluation of the ecological potential of White Sands Missile Range to support a reintroduced population of Mexican wolves. Endangered Species Report 19. U.S. Fish and Wildlife Service, Albuquerque, New Mexico. 96 pp.

Beier, P. 1993. Determining minimum habitat areas and habitat corridors for cougars. Conservation Biology: 7:94-108.

Berg, W. E., and D. W. Kuehn. 1982. Ecology of wolves in northcentral Minnesota. Pages 4 - 11 *in* F. H. Harrington, and P. C. Paquet, editors. Wolves of the world - perspectives of behaviour, ecology and management. Noyes Publications, Parks Ridge, New Jersey, USA.

Bergerud, A. T. 1985. Antipredator strategies of caribou: dispersion along coastlines. Canadian Journal of Zoology 63:1324-1329.

Bjorge, R. R., and J. R. Gunson. 1989. Wolf, *Canis lupus*, population characteristics and prey relationships near Simonette River, Alberta. Canadian Field-Naturalist 103:327-334.

Boitani, L. 1982. Wolf management in intensively used areas of Italy. Pages 158-172 *in* Harrington, F.H., and Paquet, P.C., eds. Wolves of the World. Noyes Publications, Park Ridge, N.J.

Boutin, S. 1992. Predation and moose population dynamics: a critique. Journal of Wildlife Management. 56:116-127.

Boyd, D. K. 1997. Dispersal, genetic relationships and landscape use by colonizing wolves in the central Rocky Mountains. Ph.D. thesis, University of Montana. 184 pp.

Boyd, D. K., D. H. Pletscher, R. R. Ream, and M. W. Fairchild. 1994. Prey characteristics of colonizing wolves and hunters in the Glacier National Park area. Journal of Wildlife Management. 58:289-295.

Boyd, D. K., P. C. Paquet, S. Donelon, R. R. Ream, D. H. Pletscher, and C. C. White. 1996. Transboundary movements of a recolonizing wolf population in the Rocky Mountains. Pages 135-140 in L. N. Carbyn, S. H. Fritts, and D. R. Seip, eds. Ecology and conservation of wolves in a changing world. Canadian Circumpolar Institute, University of Alberta, Edmonton, Alberta.

Brand, C. J., M. J. Pybus, W. B. Ballard, and R. O. Peterson. 1995. Infectious and parasitic diseases of the gray wolf and their potential effects on wolf populations in North America. Pages 419-429 *in* L. N. Carbyn

Breitenemoser, U., Breitenmoser-Würsten, C., Carbyn, L. N., and S. M. Funk. In press. Assessment of carnivore reintroductions.

Brown, J. H., and A. Kodric-Brown. 1977. Turnover rates in insular biogeography: effect of immigration on extinction. Ecology 58:445-449.

Burnham K.P. and D.R. Anderson. 1998. Model selection and inference, Springer Verlag New York.

Burrows, F., P. Krizan, G. Neale, and P. Paquet. 1996. Interim report on the ecology of gray wolves and associated prey species in the Greater Pukaskwa Ecosystem, Ontario, 1994-1996. Parks Canada, Heron Bay, Ontario, Canada. 93pp.

Carbyn, L. N. 1974. Wolf predation and behavioural interactions with elk and other ungulates in an area of high prey diversity. Ph.D thesis, Univ. Toronto, Toronto. 233pp.

Carbyn, L. N. 1982. Incidence of disease and its potential role in the population dynamics of wolves in Riding Mountain National Park, Manitoba. Pages 106 – 116 *in* F. H. Harrington and P.C. Paquet, editors. Wolves of the world: perspectives of behaviour, ecology, and conservation. Noyes, Park Ridge, New Jersey, USA.

Caro, T. M. and M. K. Laurenson. 1994. Ecological and genetic factors in conservation: a cautionary tale. Science 263: 465-466.

Chapman, R. C. 1977. The effects of human disturbance on wolves (*Canis lupus*). M.S. Thesis, Univ. Alaska, Fairbanks. 209pp.

Ciucci, P., L. Boitani, F. Francisci, and G. Andreoli. 1997. Home range, activity, and movements of a wolf pack in central Italy. Journal of Zoology (London) 243:803-819.

Cowan, I. McT. 1947. The timber wolf in the Rocky Mountain National Parks of Canada. Canadian Joural of Res. 25:139-174.

Curatolo, J. A. and Murphy, S. M. 1986. The effects of pipelines, roads, and traffic on the movements of caribou, *Rangifer tarandus*, Canadian Field Naturalist. 100:218-224.

Doak, D. F. 1995. Source-sink models and the problem of habitat degradation: general models and applications to the Yellowstone Grizzly. Conservation Biology. 9:1370-1379.

Duda, M. D., and K. C. Young. 1995. New Mexico resident's opinions toward Mexican wolf reintroduction. Responsive Management, Harrisonburg, Virginia. 60 pp.

East, R. 1981. Species-curves and populations of large mammals in African savanna reserves. Biological Conservation 21:111-126.

Eberhardt, L. L. 1977. Optimal policies for conservation of large mammals, with special reference to marine ecosystems. Environmental Conservation 4:205-212.

Eisenberg, J. F. 1980. The density and biomass of tropical animals. Pages 35-55 *in* M. E. Soule, and B. A. Wilcox, editors. Conservation biology: an evolutionary - ecological perspective. Sinauer Associates Incorporated, Sunderland, Massachusetts, USA.

Emmons, L. E. 1984. Geographic variation in densities and diversities of non-flying mamals in Amazonia. Biotropica 16:210-222.

Forbes, G. J., and J. B. Theberge. 1995. Influences of a migrating deer herd on wolf movements and mortality in and around Algonquin provincial park, Ontario. Pages 303-313 *in* L. N. Carbyn, S. H. Fritts, and D. R. Seip, editors. Ecology and conservation of wolves in a changing world. Canadian Circumpolar Institute, Edmonton, Alberta, Canada.

Forbes, G. J., and J. B. Theberge. 1996. Response by wolves to prey variation in central Ontario. Canadian Journal of Zoology 74:1511-1520.

Forbes, S. H. and D. K. Boyd. 1996. Genetic variation of naturally colonizing wolves in the central Rocky Mountains. Conservation Biology 10: 1082-1090.

Forbes, S. H. and D. K. Boyd. 1997. Genetic structure and migration in native and reintroduced Rocky Mountain wolf populations. Conservation Biology 11:1226-1234.

Forman, R. T. T. 1995. Land Mosaics: the ecology of landscapes and regions. Cambridge University Press, Cambridge, Mass.

Forman, R. T. and A. M. Hersperger. 1996. Road ecology and road density in different landscapes, with international planning and mitigation solutions. *In* G. L. Evink, D. Zeigler and J. Berry (eds.) Trends in addressing transportation related wildlife mortality. Florida Department of Transportation. Orlando.

Forman, R. T. T., and M. Godron. 1986. Landscape ecology. John Wiley and Sons, New York, N.Y. 619pp.

Frankel, O. H., and Soulé, M. E. 1981. Conservation and evolution. Cambridge Univ. Press, London.

Franklin, J. F. 1993. Preserving biodiversity: species, ecosystems, or landscapes. Ecological Applications. 3:202-205.

Fritts, S. H. 1983. Record dispersal by a wolf from Minnesota. Journal of Mammalogy 64:166-167.

Fritts, S. H. and L. D. Mech. 1981. Dynamics, movements and feeding ecology of a newly protected wolf population in northwestern Minnesota. Wildlife Monographs 80. 79 pp.

Fritts, S. H., and L. N. Carbyn. 1995. Population viability, nature reserves, and the outlook for gray wolf conservation in North America. Restoration Ecology 3:26-38.

Fuller, T. K., and L. B. Keith. 1980. Wolf population dynamics and prey relationships in northeastern Alberta. Journal of Wildlife Management 44:583-602.

Fuller, T. K. 1989. Population dynamics of wolves in north-central Minnesota. Wildlife Monographs 105. 41pp.

Fuller, T. K., W. E. Berg, G. L. Radde, M. S. Lenarz, and G. B. Joselyn. 1992. A history and current estimate of wolf distribution and numbers in Minnesota. Wildlife Society Bulletin. 20:42-55.

Gasaway, W. C., R. O. Stephenson, J. L. Davis, P. E. K. Shepherd, and O. E. Burris. 1983. Interrelationships of wolves, prey, and man in interior Alaska. Wildlife Monographs 84.

Gasaway, W. C., S. D. Dubois, D. J. Reed, and S. J. Harbo. 1986. Estimating moose population parameters from aerial surveys. Biological Paper 22. University of Alaska-Fairbanks, Alaska, USA. 108pp.

Gese, E. M, and L. D. Mech. 1991. Dispersal of wolves (*Canis lupus*) in northeastern Minnesota, 1969 - 1989. Canadian Journal of Zoology 69:2946-2955.

Gilpin, M. E. 1987. Spatial structure and population vulnerability. Pages 125-139 *in* Soulé, M. E., ed. Viable populations for conservation. Univ. Cambridge Press. Cambridge, Mass.

Gese, E. M, and L. D. Mech. 1991. Dispersal of wolves (*Canis lupus*) in northeastern Minnesota, 1969 - 1989. Canadian Journal of Zoology 69:2946-2955.

Glanz, W. E. 1982. The terrestrial mammal fauna of Barr Colorado Island. Census and long-term changes. Pages 239 *in* E.G. Leigh, Jr.., A.S. Rand, and D.M. Windsor, eds. The ecology of a tropical forest: seasonal rhythms and long-term changes. Smithsonian Institution Press, Washington, DC.

Green-Hammond, K. A. 1994. Assessment of impacts to populatons and humans harvests of deer and lek caused by the reintroduction of Mexican wolves. Contractor report to the U.S. Fish and Wildlife Service, Albuquerque, New Mexico. 30 pp.

Groebner, D. J., Girmendonk, A. L., and Johnson, T. B. 1995 .A proposed cooperative reintroduction plan for the Mexican wolf in Arizona. Technical Report 56. Nongame and Endangered Wildlife Program. Arizona Game and Fish Department, Phoenix, Arizona.

Gunson, J. R. 1983. Wolf-ungulate predation in North America: review of major studies. Altberta Fish and Wildlife Division Report. 31pp.

Gunson, J. R. 1992. Historical and present management of wolves in Alberta. Wildlife Society Bulletin. 20:330-339.

Hansson, L. 1991. Dispersal and connectivity in metapopulations. Pages 89 – 103 *in* M. Gilpin, and I. Hanski, editors. Metapopulation dynamics: empirical and theoretical investigations. Academic Press, New York, New York, USA.

Harris, L. D. and P. B. Gallagher. 1989. New initiatives fro wildlife conservation: the need for movement corridors. Pages 11-34 in G. MacKintosh (ed.). Preserving communities and corridors. Defenders of Wildlife, Washington, DC.

Harrison, S. 1991. Local extinction in a metapopulation context: an empirical evaluation. Pages 73-88 in M. Gilpin and L. Hanski (eds.). Metapopulation dynamics: empirical and theoretical investigations. Academic Press, New York.

Harrison, R. L. 1992. Toward a theory of inter-refuge corridor design. Conserv. Biol. 6:293-295.

Hayes, R. D., A. M. Baer, and D. G. Larsen. 1991. Population dynamics and prey relationships of an exploited and recovering wolf population in the southern Yukon. Yukon Fish and Wildlife Branch Final Report. TR-91-1. 68pp.

Hayes, R. D., and A. Harestad. 2000. Demography of a recovering wolf population in the Yukon. Canadian Journal of Zoology. 78:36-48.

Hayes, R. D., A. M. Baer, U. Wotschikowsky, and A. Harestad. 2000. Kill rate by wolves on moose in the Yukon. Canadian Journal of Zoology. 78:49-59.

Hayes, R. D., and A. Harestad. 2000. Wolf functional response and regulation of moose in the Yukon. Canadian Journal of Zoology. 78:60-66.

Heisey, D., and T. K. Fuller. 1985a. Evaluation of survival and cause-specific mortality rates using telemetry data. Journal of Wildlife Management. 49:668-674.

Heisey, D., and T. K. Fuller. 1985b. MICROMORT user's guide. Forest and Wildlife Population and Research Group, Grand Rapids, Minnesota.

Henry, V. G. 1995. Revision of the special rule for nonessential experimental populations of red wolves in North Carolina and Tennessee – final rule. Federal Register 60:18940-18948.

Holling, C. S. 1973. Resilience and stability of ecological systems. Annual Review of Ecology and Systematics. 4:1-23.

Holroyd, G. L. and K. J. Van Tighem. 1983. Ecological (biophysical) land classification of Banff and Jasper National Parks. Volume III: the wildlife inventory. Canadian Wildlife Service, Edmonton. 691 pp.

Huggard, D. J. 1991. Prey selectivity of wolves in Banff National Park. M.Sc. Thesis. Univ. B.C., Vancouver, B.C. 119pp.

Huggard, D. J. 1993a. Effect of snow depth on predation and scavenging by gray wolves. Journal of Wildlife Management. 57:382-388.

Huggard, D. J. 1993b. Prey selectivity of wolves in Banff National Park, I. Age, sex, and condition of elk. Canadian Journal of Zoology. 71:130-139.

Huggard, D. J. 1993c. Prey selectivity of wolves in Banff National Park, II. Age, sex, and condition of elk. Canadian Journal of Zoology. 71:140-147.

IUCN. 1994. Red list categories. (www.iucn.org/themes/ssc/redlists/ssc-rl-c.htm

Jalkotzy, M. G., P. I. Ross and M. D. Nasserden. 1997. The effects of linear developments on wildlife: a review of selected scientific literature. Prepared for Canadian Association of Petroleum Producers. Calgary. 224 pp.

Janz, B. and D. Storr. 1977. The climate of the contiguous mountain parks. Atmospheric Environment Services, Toronto. Project report No. 30. 324 pp.

Jenkins, K.J., and R.G. Wright. 1988. Resource partitioning and competition among cervids in the Northern Rocky Mountains. Journal of Applied Ecology. 25:11-24.

Jensen, W. F.; Fuller, T. K.; Robinson, W. L. 1986. Wolf, *Canis lupus*, distribution on the Ontario-Michigan border near Sault Ste. Marie. Canandian Field Naturalist.

Kaplan, E. L. and P. Meier. 1958. Nonparmetric estimation from incomplete observations. Journal of American Statistics Association 53:475-481.

Kay, C. E. 1990. Yellowstone's northern elk herd: a critical evaluation of the "natural regulation" paradigm. Ph.D. Thesis, Utah State Univ., Logan. 490 pp.

Kay, C. E. and F. H. Wagner. 1994. Historic condition of woody vegetation on Yellowstone's northern range: a critical test of the "natural regulation paradigm. Pp. 159-169 *in* D. Despain, ed. Plants and their environment. Proc. First Bienn. Conf. Greater Yellowstone ecosystem. U.S. Natl. Park Serv. Tech. Rep.

Keith, L. B. 1983. Population dynamics of wolves. Pages 66 – 77 *in* L. N. Carbyn, editor. Wolves in Canada and Alaska: Their Status, Biology and Management. Canadian Wildlife Service Report Series Number 45, Edmonton, AB.

Keller, V. and H. P. Pfister. 1995. Wildlife passages as a means of mitigating effects of habitat fragmentation by roads and railway lines. *In* Habitat fragmentation and infrastructure. Proceedings of the international conference: habitat fragmentation, infrastructure and the role of ecological engineering, 17 – 21 September, 1995. Naastricht, The Hague, The Netherlands. 474 pp.

Kenward, R. E., and K. H. Hodder. 1996. RANGES V: An analysis system for biological data. Institute of Terrestrial Ecology, Furzebrook Research Station, Wareham, Dorset, England, UK. 66pp.

Kolenosky, G. B., and D. H. Johnston. 1967. Radio-tracking timber wolves in Ontario. American Zoologist 7:289-303.

Kolenosky, G. B. 1972. Wolf predation on wintering deer in east-central Ontario. Journal of Wildlife Management 36:357-369.

Klein, D. R. 1995. The introduction, increase, and demise of wolves on Coronation Island, Alaska. *In* Carbyn, L. N., S. H. Fritts, D. R. Seip (*Eds.*). Ecology and conservation of wolves in a changing world. Canadian Circumpolar Institute, University of Alberta. Edmonton, AB.

Kolenosky, G. B., and D. H. Johnston. 1967. Radio-tracking timber wolves in Ontario. American Zoologist 7:289-303.

Krizan, P. 1997. The effects of human development, landscape features, and prey density on the spatial use of wolves *(Canis lupus)* on the north shore of Lake Superior. M. S. Thesis. Center for Wildlife and Conservation Biology, Acadia University, Wolfville, Nova Scotia, Canada. 109pp.

Land, D. and M. Lotz. 1996. Wildlife crossing design and use by Florida panthers and other wildlife in southwest Florida. *In* G. L. Evink, D. Zeigler and J. Berry (eds.) Trends in addressing transportation related wildlife mortality. Florida Department of Transportation. Orlando.

Larkin R. P. 1996. Effects of military noise on wildlife. USACERL Technical Report 96/21. 219 pp.

Leeson, B. 1996. Highway conflicts and resolutions in Banff National Park, Alberta. *In* G. L. Evink, D. Zeigler and J. Berry (eds.) Trends in addressing transportation related wildlife mortality. Florida Department of Transportation, Orlando.

Leigh, E.G., S.J. Wright, E.A. Herre, and F.E. Putz. 1993. The decline of tree diversity on newly isolated tropical islands: a test of a null hypothesis and some implications. Evolutionary Ecology 7:76-102.

Lovejoy, T. E., R. O. Bierregaard Jr., A. B. Rylands, J. R. Malcolm, C. E. Quintela, L. H. Harper, K. S. Brown Jr., A. H. Powell, G. V. N. Powell, H. O. R. Schubart and M. B. Hays. 1986. Edge and other effects of isolation on Amazon forest fragments. Pages 257-285 *in* Conservation biology: The science of scarcity and diversity. Sinauer Associates., Sunderland, MA.

McLaren, B. E., and R. O. Peterson. 1994. Wolves, moose, and tree rings on Isle Royale. Science 266:1555-1558.

Meadows, B. 2001. Southern Rockies wildlife and wilderness survey report. Decision Research, Washington, D.C. 121 pp.

Mech, L. D. 1970. The wolf: the ecology and behavior of an endangered species. The Natural History Press, Garden City, New York. 384pp.

Mech, L. D. 1973. Wolf numbers in the Superior National Forest of Minnesota. United States Forest Service Research Report. NC-07. 10pp.

Mech, L. D. 1977a. Productivity, mortality, and population trends of wolves in northeastern Minnesota. Journal of Mammalogy 58:559-574.

Mech, L. D. 1977b. Population trend and winter deer consumption in a Minnesota wolf pack. Pages 55-74 *in* R. L. Phillips and C. Jonkel, editors. Proceedings of the 1975 predator symposium. Montana Forest and Conservation Experiment Station, University of Montana, Missoula, Montana, USA. 268pp.

Mech, L. D. 1986. Wolf population in the central Superior National Forest, 1967-1985. USDA Forest Service Research Paper. NC-270. 6pp.

Mech, L. D. 1989. Wolf population survival in an area of high road density. Amer. Midl. Nat. 121:387 - 389.

Mech, L. D. 1991. The way of the wolf. Voyageur press, Stillwater, Minnesota, USA. 120pp.

Mech, L. D. 1993. Updating our thinking on the role of human activity in wolf recovery. Research information bulletin 57. U.S. Fish and Wildlife Service. St. Paul, Minnesota.

Mech, L. D. 1995. The challenge and opportunity of recovering wolf populations. Conservation Biology 9: 270 - 278.

Mech, L. D. 1996. A new era for carnivore conservation. Wildlife Society Bulletin 24: 397 - 401.

Mech, L.D. and P. D. Karns. 1977. Role of the wolf in a deer decline in the Superior National Forest. U.S. Dept. Agricul. For. Serv., Res. Pap. NC-143. 23pp.

Mech, L. D., S. H. Fritts, G. L. Radde, and W. J. Paul. 1988. Wolf distribution and road density in Minnesota. Wildlife Society Bulleting. 16:85-87.

Mech, L. D. and S. M. Goyal. 1993. Canine parvovirus effect on wolf population change and pup survival. Journal of Wildlife Diseases. 22:104-106.

Meidinger, D. and J. Pojar (eds.). 1991. Ecosystems of British Columbia. British Columbia Ministry of Forests. Special Report Series No. 6. Victoria. 330 pp.

Meier, T. J., J. W. Burch, L. D. Mech, and L. G. Adams. 1995. Pack structure and genetic relatedness among wolf packs in a naturally-regulated population. Pages 293-302 *in* L. N. Carbyn, S. H. Fritts, and D. R . Seip, editors. Ecology and conservation of wolves in a changing world. Canadian Circumpolar Institute, Edmonton, Alberta, Canada.

Merriam, G., and A. Lanoue. 1990. Corridor use by small mammals: field measurements for three experimental types of *Peromyscus leucopus*. Landscape Ecology 4:123-131.

Merrill,S. B. 2000. Road densities and Wolf, Canis lupus, habitat suitability:an exception. Canadian Field Naturalist 114:312-314.

Messier, F. 1984. Moose-wolf dynamics and the natural regulation of moose populations. Ph. D. Thesis, University of British Columbia, Vancouver, British Columbia, Canada. 143pp.

Messier, F. 1985a. Social organization, spatial distribution, and population density of wolves in relation to moose density. Canadian Journal of Zoology 63:1068-1077.

Messier, F. 1985b. Solitary living and extraterritorial movements of wolves in relation to social status and prey abundance. Canadian Journal of Zoology 63:239-245.

Messier, F. 1987. Physical condition and blood physiology of wolves in relation to moose density. Canadian Journal of Zoology 65:91-95.

Messier, F. 1991. The significance of limiting and regulating factors on the demography of moose and white-tailed deer. Journal of Animal Ecology 60:377-393.

Messier, F. 1994. Ungulate population models with predation: a case study with the North American moose. Ecology 75:478-488.

Messier, F., and C. Barrette. 1985. The efficiency of yarding behavior by white-tailed deer as an anti-predatory strategy. Canadian Journal of Zoology. 63:785-789.

Messier, F. and M. Crête. 1985. Moose-wolf dynamics and the natural regulation of moose populations. Oecologica. 65:503-512.

Mladenoff, D. J. , T. A. Sickley, R. G. Haight, A. P. Wydeven.. 1995. A regional landscape analysis and prediction of favorable gray wolf habitat in the northern Great Lakes region. Conservation Biology. 9:279 - 294.

Mladenoff, D. J., R. G. Haight, T. A. Sickley, and A. P. Wydeven. 1997. Causes and implications of species restoration in altered ecosystems: a spatial landscape projection of wolf population recovery. Bioscience 47:21-31.

Mladenoff, D. J. and T. A. Sickley. 1998. Assessing potential gray wolf restoration in the Northeastern United States: a spatial prediction of favorable habitat and population level. JWM 62:1-10.

Mohr, C. O. 1947. Table of equivalent populations of North American small mammals. American Midland Naturalist 37:223-249.

Nams, V. O., and Boutin, S. 1991. What is wrong with error polygons? Journal of Wildlife Management 55:172-176.

Murie, A. 1944. The wolves of Mount McKinley. Fauna of the National Parks of the United States. Fauna Series No. 5. U.S. Govt. Printing Office, Wash, D.C. 238pp.

Nelson, M. E., and L. D. Mech. 1981. Deer social organization and wolf predation in northeastern Minnesota. Wildlife Monograph. 77:1-53.

Nelson, M. E. and L. D. Mech. 1986. Relationship between snow depth and gray wolf predation on white-tailed deer. J. Wildl. Mange. 50:471-474.

Nelson, M. E. and Mech, L. D. 1986. Mortality of white-tailed deer in northeastern Minnesota. Journal of Wildlife Management. 50:691-698.

Noss, R. F. 1991. Landscape connectivity: different functions at different scales. Pp. 27-39 *In* W. E. Hudson (ed.). Landscape linkages and biodiversity. Island Press, Washington.

Noss, R. F. 1992. The wildlands project land conservation strategy. Pp. 10 – 25 *In* Wild Earth (special issue), Plotting a North American wilderness recovery strategy. The Wildlands Project. Canton, N. Y. 88 pp.

Noss, R. F. 1993. Wildlife corridors. In D.S. Smith and P.A. Hellmund, eds. Ecology of Greenways. University of Minnesota Press, Minneapolis, MN.

Noss, R. F. 1995. Maintaining ecological integrity in representative reserve networks. A World Wildlife Fund Canada/World Wildlife Fund United States Discussion Paper. Toronto, Ontario, Canada, and Washington, DC, USA.

Noss, R. F., H. B. Quigley, M. G. Hornocker, T. Merrill, and P. C. Paquet. 1996. Conservation biology and carnivore conservation in the Rocky Mountains. Conservation Biology 10:949-963.

Okarma, H., W. Jedrzejewski, K. Schmidt, S. Sniezko, A. N. Bonevich,, and B. Jedrzejewska. 1998. Home ranges of wolves in Bialowieza Primeval Forest, Poland, compared with other Eurasian populations. Journal of Mammalogy 79:842-952.

Oosenberg, S. M., and L. N. Carbyn. 1982. Winter predation on bison and activity patterns of a wolf pack in Wood Buffalo National Park. Pages 43-53 *in* F. H. Harrington and P. C. Paquet, editors. Wolves: a worldside perspective of their behaviour, ecology and conservation. Noyes Publications, Park Ridge, New Jersey, USA.

Oxley, D. J., Fenton, M. B., and Carmody, G. R. 1984. The effects of roads on populations of small mammals. J. Appl. Ecol. 2:51-59.

Packard, J. M., and L. D. Mech. 1980. Population regulation in wolves. Pages 35-150 *in* M. N. Cohen, R. S. Malpass, and H. G. Klein, editors. Biosocial mechanisms of population regulation. Yale University Press, New Haven, Connecticut, USA, and London, England, UK.

Paine, R. T. 1966. Food web complexity and species diversity. American Naturalist. 100:65-75.

Paine, R. T. 1969. A note on trophic complexity and community stability. American. Naturalist. 103:91-93.

Paine, R. T. 1980. Food webs: linkage, interaction strength and community infrastructure. Journal of. Animal Ecology. 49:667-685.

Paquet, P. C. 1993. Summary reference document - ecological studies of recolonizing wolves in the Central Canadian Rocky Mountains. Unpublished Report by John/Paul and Assoc. for Canadian Parks Service, Banff, AB. 176pp.

Paquet, P. C., and A. Hackman. 1995. Large carnivore conservation in the Rocky Mountains: a long-term strategy for maintaining free-ranging and self-sustaining populations of carnivores. World Wildlife Fund-Canada. Toronto, Ontario, Canada. 53pp.

Paquet, P. C., J. Wierchowski, and C. Callaghan. 1996. Effects of human activity on gray wolves in the Bow River valley. Banff National Park, Banff, Alberta, Canada. 113pp. + maps.

Paquet, P. C. and C. Callaghan. 1996. Effects of linear developments on winter movements of gray wolves in the Bow River Valley of Banff National Park, Alberta. *In* G. L. Evink, D. Zeigler and J. Berry (eds.) Trends in addressing transportation related wildlife mortality. Florida Department of Transportation. Orlando.

Paquet, P. C., J. Wierzchowski and C. Callaghan. 1996. Summary report on the effects of human activity on gray wolves in the Bow River Valley, Banff National Park, Alberta. Chapter 7 *In*: Green, J., C. Pacas, S. Bayley and L. Cornwell (eds.). A Cumulative Effects Assessment and

Futures Outlook for the Banff Bow Valley. Prepared for the Banff Bow Valley Study, Department of Canadian Heritage, Ottawa, ON.

Paquet, P. C., J. Wierzchowski and C. Callaghan. 1999. Summary document of wolf ecology in Kootenay and Yoho National Parks. Prepared for Parks Canada.

Parks Canada. 1994. Initial assessment of proposed improvements to the TransCanada highway in Banff National Park IIIA, Sunshine Interchange to Castle Mountain Interchange. Calgary, Alberta, Canada.

Parsons, D. R. 1998. Endangered and threatened wildlife and plants; establishment of a nonessential experimental population of the Mexican wolf in Arizona and New Mexico: final rule. Federal Register 63:1752-1772

Pate, J., M. J. Manfredo, A. D. Bight, and G. Tischbein. 1996. Coloradan's attitudes toward reintroducing the gray wolf into Colorado. Wildlife Society Bulletin 24:421-428.

Person, D. K. 2000. Wolves, deer and logging: Population viability and predator-prey dynamics in a disturbed insular landscape. PhD Thesis. University of Alaska, Fairbanks, AK.

Person, D. K., M. Kirchoff, V. Van Ballenberghe, G. C. Iverson and E. Grossman. 1996. The Alexander Archipelago wolf: a conservation assessment. United States Department of Agriculture - Forest Service. General Technical Report. PNW-GTR-384.

Person, D. K. and M. A. Ingle. 1995. Ecology of the Alexander Achipelago wolf and responses to habitat change. Progress Report Number 3. Alaska Department of Fish and Game. Douglas, AK.

Peterson, R. L. 1977. Wolf ecology and prey relationships on Isle Royale. United States National Park Service Scientific Monograph Series 11:1-210.

Peterson, R. O., J. D. Woolington, and T. N. Bailey. 1984. Wolves of the Kenai Peninsula, Alaska. Wildlife Monographs 88.

Peterson, R. O., J. D. Woolington and T. N. Bailey. 1984. Wolves of the Kenai Peninsula, Alaska. Wildlife Monographs 88: 1 – 52.

Peterson, R. O., and R. E. Page. 1988. The rise and fall of Isle Royale wolves, 1975-1986. Journal of Mammalogy 69:89-99.

Phillips, M. K., and D. W. Smith. 1998. Gray wolves and private landowners in the Greater Yellowstone Area. Transactions of the North American Wildlife and Natural Resources Conference 63:443-450.

Pickett, S. T. A., J. Kolasa, J. J. Armesto, and S. L. Collins. 1989. The ecological concept of disturbance and its expression at various hierarchical levels. Oikos 54:129-136.

Pimlott, D. 1967. Wolf predation and ungulate populations. American Zoologist 7:267-278.

Pletscher, D. H., R. R. Ream, D. K. Boyd, M. W. Fairchild, and K. E. Kunkel. 1997. Population dynamics of a recolonizing wolf population. Journal of Wildlife Management 61:459-465.

Potvin, F. 1987. Wolf movements and population dynamics in Papineau-Labelle reserve, Quebec. Canadian Journal of Zoology 66:1266-1273.

Purves, H. D., White, C. A., and Paquet, P. C. 1992. Wolf and grizzly bear habitat use and displacement by human use in Banff, Yoho, and Kootenay National Parks: a preliminary analysis. Canadian Parks Service Reptort. Banff, Alta. 54pp.

Rausch, R. A. 1967. Some aspects of the population ecology of wolves, Alaska. American Zoologist 7:253-265.

Ream, R. R., M. W. Fairchild, D. K. Boyd, and D. H. Pletscher. 1991. Population dynamics and home range changes in a colonizing wolf population. Pages 349-366 in R. B. Keiter and M. S. Boyce, eds. The greater Yellowstone ecosystem: redefining America's wilderness heritage. Yale University Press, New Haven, CT.

Refsnider, R. 2000. Endangered and threatened wildlife and plants; proposal to reclassify and remove the gray wolf from the list of endangered and threatened wildlife in the conterminous United States; proposal to establish three special regulations for threatened gray wolves. Federal Register 65:43450-43496.

Schonewald-Cox, C. M., S. M. Chambers, B. MacBryde, and L. Thomas. 1983. Genetics and conservation: a reference for managing wild animal and plant populations. Benjamin-Cummings, Menlo Park, CA.

Schonewald-Cox, C. M., and M. Buechner. 1992. Park protection and public roads. Pages 373-396 *in* P. L. Fiedler and S. K. Jain (eds.), Conservation biology: The theory and practice of nature conservation, preservation and management. Chapman and Hall, New York.

Shaffer, M. 1987. Minimum viable populations: coping with uncertainty. Pages 69-87 in M. Soule, ed. Viable populations for conservation. Cambridege University Press, New York, New York.

Sih, A., P. Crowley, M. McPeek, J. Petranka, and K. Strohmeier. 1985. Predation, competition, and prey communities: a review of field experiments. Ann. Rev. Ecol. Syst. 16:269-311.

Simberloff, D. 1998. Flagships, umbrellas, and keystones: Is single-species management passe in the landscape era? Biological Conservation 83:247 – 257.

Singer, F. J. 1979. Status and history of the timber wolves in Glacier National Park, Montana. Pages 19-42 *in* E. Klinghammer (ed.). The bheavior and ecology of wolves. Garland STPM Press, N.Y.

Singleton, P. H.. 1995. Winter habitat selection by wolves in the North Fork of the Flathead River Basin, Montana and British Columbia. M.Sc. Thesis, Univeristy of Montana, Missoula.116 pp.

Soulé, M. E. 1980. Thresholds for survival: maintaining fitness and evolutionary potential. Pages 151-169 *In* M. E. Soulé and B. A. Wilcox (eds.), Conservation biology: an ecological-evolutionary perspective. Sinauer Associates, Sunderland, MA.

Soulé, M. E. and D. Simberloff. 1986. What do genetics and ecology tell us about the design of nature reserves? Biological Conservation. 35:19-40.

Soulé, M. A. 1987. Viable populations for conservation. Cambridge University Press, New York.

Stephens, P. W. and R. O. Peterson. 1987. Wolf avoidance strategies of moose. Holacrtic Ecology 7:239-244.

Terborgh, J. 1988. The big things that run the world - a sequel to E. O. Wilson. Conservation Biology 2: 402-403.

Terborgh, J., and B. Winter. 1980. Some causes of extinction. Pages 119-134 *in* M.E. Soulé and Wilcox, B.A., eds., Conservation biology: an evolutionary-ecological perspective. Sinauer Assoc., Sunderland, Mass.

Terborgh, J., J. Estes, P. Paquet, K. Ralls, D. Boyd-Heger, B. Miller and R. Noss. 1999. The role of top carnivores in regulating terrestrial ecosystems. Wild Earth 9:42–56.

Thiel, R. P. 1985. Relationship between road densities and wolf habitat suitability in Wisconsin, American Midland Naturalist 113:404-407.

Thiel, R. P., S. Merrill and L. D. Mech. 1998. Tolerance by denning wolves, *Canis lupus*, to human disturbance. Canadian Field Naturalist 112: 340 - 342.

Thiel, R. P., and J. Valen. 1995. Developing a state timber wolf recovery plan with public input: the Wisconsin experience. Pages 169-175 *in* L. N. Carbyn, S. H. Fritts, and D. R. Seip, editors. Ecology and conservation of wolves in a changing world. Canadian Circumpolar Institute, Edmonton, Alberta, Canada.

Thurber, J. M.; Peterson, R. O.; Drummer, T. D.; Thomasma, S. A. 1994. Gray wolf response to refuge boundaries and roads in Alaska. Wildlife Society Bulletin. 22:61-68.

Thurber, J. M., and R. O. Peterson. 1993. Effects of population density and pack size on the foraging ecology of gray wolves. Journal of Mammalogy 74:879-889.

Trainer, C. E., J. C. Lemos, T. P. Kristner, W. C. Lightfoot, and D. C. Toweill. 1981. Mortality of mule deer fawns in southeastern Oregon. 1968-1979. Oregon Department of Fish Wildlife., Wildlife Restoration. Report 10. 113pp.

Trent, T. T., and O. J. Rongstad. 1974. Home range and survival of cottontail rabbits in southwestern Wisconsin. Journal of Wildlife Management. 47:716-728.

U.S. Fish and Wildlife Service. 1996. Reintroduction of the Mexican wolf within its historic range in the southwestern United States - final environmental impact statement. U.S. Fish and Wildlife Service, Albuquerque, New Mexico.

U.S. Fish and Wildlife Service. 1982. Mexican wolf recovery plan. U.S. Fish and Wildlife Service, Albuquerque, New Mexico. 115 pp.

Van Ballenberghe, V., and L. D. Mech. 1975. Weights, growth, and survival of timber wolf pups in Minnesota. Journal of Mammalogy 56:44-63.

Van Ballenberghe, V., A.. W. Erickson and D. Byman. 1975. Ecology of the timber wolf in northeastern Minnesota. Wildlife Monographs. Vol. 43. 43 pp.

Van Ballenberghe, V. 1981. Population dynamics of wolves in the Nelchina Basin, southcentral Alaska. Pages 1246-1258 *in* J. A. Chapman, and D. Pursley, editors. Worldwide Furbearer Conference, Frostburg, Maryland, USA.

Waters, D. 1988. Monitoring program mitigative measures. Canadian Parks Service, Banff National Park Warden Service Report. 57 pp.

Weaver, J. L., P. C. Paquet, and L. F. Ruggiero. 1996. Resilience and conservation of large carnivores in the Rocky Mountains. Conservation Biology 10:964-976.

Weaver, J. L. 1994. Ecology of wolf predation amidst high ungulate diversity in Jasper National Park, Alberta. PhD thesis. University of Montana, Missoula. 166pp.

White, G. C., and R. A. Garrot. 1990. Analysis of wildlife radio-tracking data. Academic Press Limited, San Diego, California, USA. 383pp.

White, C.A., P. C. Paquet, and H. D. Purves. 1992. Nursing Humpty's syndrome: Bow Valley ecosystem restoration. Paper presented at the Society for Ecological Restoration, Fourth Annual

Conference. 10-14 August, University of Waterloo, Waterloo, ON.

White, G. C. 2000 MARK (software) Www.cnr.colostate.edu/~gwhite/mark/mark.htm

Wilcove, D. S., McLellan, C. H., and Dobson, A. P. 1986. Habitat fragmentation in the temperate zone. Pages 237-256 in Soulé, M. E., ed. Conservation biology: the science of scarcity and diversity. Sinauer Associates. Sunderland, Mass.

Wilcox, B. A., and Murphy, D.D. 1985. The effects of fragmentation on extinction. Am. Naturalist 125:879-887.

Wilson, P. J., Grewal, S., Lawford, I. D., Heal, J., Granacki, A. G., Pennock, D., Theberge, J. B., Theberge, M. T., Voigt, D., Waddell, W., Chambers, R. E., Paquet, P. C., Goulet, G., Cluff, D., and B. N. White. 2000. DNA profiles of the eastern Canadian wolf and the red wolf provide evidence for a common evolutionary history independent of the gray wolf. Canadian Journal of Zool.78:2156 - 2166

Wright, S. 1977. Evolution and the genetics of populations. Vol. 3. Univ. of Chicago Press, Chicago.

Wydeven, A. P., R. N. Schultz, and R. P. Thiel. 1995. Monitoring of a recovering wolf population in Wisconsin, 1979 – 1991. Pages 147-156 *in* L. N. Carbyn, S. H. Fritts, and D. R. Seip, editors. Ecology and conservation of wolves in a changing world. Canadian Circumpolar Institute, Edmonton, Alberta

Wydeven, A. P., R. N. Schultz, and R. P. Thiel. 1995. Monitoring of a recovering wolf population in Wisconsin, 1979 – 1991. Pages 147-156 *in* L. N. Carbyn, S. H. Fritts, and D. R. Seip, editors. Ecology and conservation of wolves in a changing world. Canadian Circumpolar Institute, Edmonton, Alberta

Young, S. P. and E. A. Goldman. 1944. Wolves of North America. Dover Publications. New York. NY.